Compliments of

John Gasdaska
Licensed Associate Real Estate Broker
Tel: 646.345.7350
jwg@corcoran.com

Jonathan Conlon
Licensed Associate Real Estate Broker
Tel: 347.564.2440
jconlon@corcoran.com

The Gasdaska Conlon Team
Corcoran - 660 Madison Avenue, NYC 10065

CITY GREEN

Public Gardens of New York

CITY GREEN
Public Gardens of New York

Jane Garmey

Photographs by Mick Hales

THE MONACELLI PRESS

Contents

Introduction

Never doubt that a small group of thoughtful, committed citizens can change the world. Indeed, it is the only thing that ever has.

— Margaret Mead

New Yorkers hold strong views about their city. They will discuss buildings, museums, and neighborhoods, and they love to give their opinions on restaurants, traffic, baseball teams, subways, potholes, and politicians. Gardens, however, are not usually a part of their discourse. Everyone loves Central Park, the High Line ranks as the city's second largest tourist attraction, and the New York Botanical Garden (NYBG) is acknowledged as one of the world's pre-eminent botanical gardens. But, ask about other public gardens and, more often than not, the response is vague.

This is surprising because there are a lot of public parks and gardens within the five boroughs of New York. *City Green* is a selective survey of gardens, not parks. The difference between the two is subtle, but it comes down to scale and purpose. Parks are typically larger than gardens and intended to be used as recreational space. Gardens, which can stand alone or be within a park or botanical garden, are designed and intended for the growth and enjoyment of plants and trees. Distinctions, however, can get blurred when public gardens incorporate cultural and social activities into their agenda.

My choice of New York public gardens may seem idiosyncratic, but my intention is to present a rich diversity. So, in addition to traditional gardens like Wave Hill, formerly a private estate in Riverdale, and Beatrice Farrand's rose garden at NYBG, I feature such contemporary gardens as Louis Kahn's minimalist Four Freedoms Park on Roosevelt Island and Michael Van Valkenburgh's wild garden within Brooklyn Bridge Park. Also included are three examples of community gardens, a garden created in a historic city square, and gardens with a particular raison d'étre, such as the re-creation of three medieval monastic gardens at the Cloisters, Noguchi's sculpture garden in Queens, and a rooftop farm garden at the Brooklyn Navy Yard.

Some years ago, I received an assignment from the *Wall Street Journal* to write about the reclamation of The Battery at the tip of Lower Manhattan. I became fascinated by the story of how this garden had been raised like Lazarus from the dead, and it made me curious to learn more about the history and vicissitudes of other public gardens. Over the years, I became familiar with more city gardens and wrote about some of them. However, it was a chance visit to the beautiful and little-known Heather Garden at Fort Tryon Park that triggered the idea for this book.

Promenade at The Battery.

In doing research, I discovered that many of the city's older gardens would not have survived without the often-Herculean efforts of a few individuals. Their stories intrigued me. During the 1970s when New York was in fiscal chaos and came close to bankruptcy, nearly every garden took a hit as the Parks Department was in free-fall, with its budget in shreds and services cut to the bone. The first most visible angel to appear was urban planner, writer, and activist Elizabeth Barlow Rogers. She was appointed Central Park's first administrator in 1979 and a year later initiated the Central Park Conservancy, a private non-profit organization set up to work in partnership with the Parks Department to restore Central Park.

In 1982 Rogers recruited artist-turned-horticulturist Lynden Miller to take on the restoration of the Conservatory Garden at the north end of Central Park. It was overgrown, strewn with garbage, and considered one of the most dangerous places in the park. Although she had never designed a public garden, Miller, who also raised the funds needed for the restoration, created what is generally agreed to be Manhattan's most beautiful formal garden. She has gone on to become a renowned designer and tireless advocate of public gardens.

In the early 1990s, Warrie Price, also a Rogers protégée, accepted the challenge of restoring the gardens at The Battery, inviting Piet Oudolf to create a horticultural plan for what was a desolate down-at-the heels eyesore and setting up the Battery Park Conservancy (a non-profit organization similar

Preceding spread: Westside Community Garden.

Conservatory Garden,
Central Park.

Heather Garden, Fort
Tryon Park.

to the Central Park Conservancy). Today, The Battery has been transformed beyond recognition.

Bette Midler is another of New York's garden angels. Moving back to the city in 1995, she organized her friends to clean up the neglect and mess of Fort Tryon and Fort Washington Parks. This led to the founding of the New York Restoration Project which, in 1999, was instrumental in saving 114 city-owned parks that had been put up for sale by Mayor Rudolph Giuliani. Today the organization is responsible for the care and maintenance of 52 of these gardens, and is actively engaged in preserving community gardens and revitalizing green space in all of New York's boroughs.

There are countless other success stories. When Gregory Long became president of NYBG in 1988, its operating budget was larger than its endowment, its historic glass conservatory was in desperate need of restoration, and its plant and tree collections languished as a backdrop for what had become a giant dog run. Today NYBG is an important cultural destination, with more than 1.1 million visitors coming each year to see and enjoy thirteen display gardens, several specialized tree collections, and seasonal exhibitions in the restored conservatory. Many of these shows are accompanied by professionally curated art exhibits. This concept of presenting horticulture within a larger cultural context has been pioneered and developed by NYBG. The Garden also offers a full complement of professional and public educational programs and has the most extensive herbarium and botanical horticultural library in the world

Other survival stories pre-date the city's financial crisis. Wave Hill would not be a public garden today without the efforts of a group of Riverdale residents, who came together in 1963 and were able to stop the rampant over-development of historic Riverdale by getting the zoning changed. And one of the city's most unusual gardens, the Chinese Scholar's Garden at Staten Island's Snug Harbor Cultural Center and Botanic Garden, exists thanks to Frances X. Paolo Huber, who thought up the idea, raised the necessary public and private funds, persuaded the Chinese Government to support the cost of fabrication, and even organized housing for the thirty craftsmen who came from China to construct the garden.

Community gardens are an increasingly visible kind of public garden, and they frequently play a crucial role in the growth and improvement of a neighborhood. New York has more than 500 of community gardens and the West Side Community Garden is one of the earliest examples of how much can be accomplished by a small group of citizens. In 1975 a cadre of Upper West Side residents were so frustrated by the rubble of a failed urban development project taking up an entire city block that they occupied the site and then got permission from their local community board to create a temporary community garden. Seven years later, when the building project started up again, they negotiated a settlement with the city to retain and take ownership of part of the site and persuaded the developer to pay for the design of a new garden. Since then, this group has become a non-profit organization and has assumed all responsibility for upkeep and maintenance.

New York Chinese
Scholar's Garden.

Today, this garden is not only enjoyed for its horticultural charms but has become a nexus for cultural events and social gatherings. This has also happened with many other community gardens. A good example is the Community Garden District, a network of 39 gardens that have grown up in and around the tenement buildings on the Lower East Side, which has become the social and cultural hub of a historically Latino neighborhood now engulfed by rapid gentrification.

Most community gardens are maintained by volunteers but, unlike the West Side Community Garden which owns its land, their space is subject to renewable leases from the city. Rapidly rising real estate prices on the Lower East Side has residents fearful that their gardens will be seen as potential development sites. Another worry is that as available land becomes increasingly scarce, the city may decide to raze community gardens to use as affordable housing sites.

High Line.

Brooklyn Bridge Park.

Acknowledgement that New York is a city of islands has been slow in coming, but finally the city's shoreline is getting the attention it deserves. Brooklyn Bridge Park, an ambitious undertaking to redefine a large part of Brooklyn's waterfront, is the most prominent example of this new way of thinking. Other exciting new park developments are Governor's Island and Hudson River Park, a waterfront park extending from 59th Street to Battery Park. Close to completion, it already offers opportunities for biking, sailing, and paddle boating.

Gardens and parks are not a luxury but an essential part of what makes a city livable, and it is now recognized that imaginative and well-designed outdoor space brings a city immeasurable benefits—economic, cultural, and recreational. The High Line is the most visible example of this understanding, but it too would not have happened but for the chance meeting of two Chelsea residents at a community board meeting. Inspired by the High Line, there is now a plan to turn a unused three-and-a-half-mile stretch of the Rockaway Beach branch of the Long Island Rail Road into a linear garden walkway.

The ever-growing appreciation of New York's parks and gardens tells a story of how green has triumphed over tarmac and plants over weeds. The bad old days of neglect are no more at the Parks Department, and the public private-partnership funding model, so successfully developed by the Central Park Conservancy, is now replicated, with variations, in many public gardens. Demographics tell us that more and more people are choosing to live in cities. They jog, bike, walk, take their children out to play, frequent green markets, meet friends for picnics and outdoor events, and they are vocal advocates for grass, plants, trees, water, and clean air. Their insistence that the outdoors be an essential part of their urban experience has become a driving force behind the development of new parks and gardens, and the better care and improvement of those that already exist. City green has come of age.

Green-Wood

Brooklyn

Green-Wood Cemetery is remarkable not only for its ornate statuary and exotic mausoleums but also for its sylvan beauty, glorious trees, and rich variety of bird life. This cemetery in a garden was founded in 1838, a time of rapid urbanization, when churchyards were literally running out of burial space. As one of the first rural cemeteries in America, Green-Wood was a response to this situation and also served as a catalyst for the adoption of an English landscape style in a new kind of garden-like burial ground. In addition, it became the impetus and inspiration for the creation of Central Park.

The cemetery was founded on 178 acres of Brooklyn farmland by Henry Evelyn Pierrepont, who was inspired by a visit to Mount Auburn Cemetery in Cambridge, Massachusetts. He assembled the land and hired civil engineer David Bates Douglass to work on its layout and design.

Native vegetation was preserved and augmented with groves of trees by Almerin Hotchkiss, superintendent of grounds, who took the helm after Douglass. In places the terrain rose to two hundred feet above sea level, making it the highest point of land in Brooklyn and offering breathtaking views of New York Harbor. Douglass's plan called for an intricate network of drives and paths to follow the natural contours of the land and wind in a maze-like fashion around the hills, valleys, lakes, and wooded areas of the site.

With its classical monuments and extravagant Gothic Revival mausoleums rising out of the open landscape, Green-Wood marked a distinct break with colonial-era burying grounds and church-affiliated graveyards. The advent of a naturalistic burial ground coincided with the rising popularity of the word "cemetery," derived from the Greek word meaning "a sleeping place" and signifying a new, gentler view of death and the afterlife.

By the early 1850s, Green-Wood was receiving acolades for its open space and natural beauty and was attracting more than 500,000 visitors a year, second only to Niagara Falls as the nation's most popular tourist attraction. It was not just a prestigious place to be buried, but it also became a destination for family outings, picnics, carriage rides, and to view its ever-growing collection of statuary and ornate mausoleums.

In 1849 Andrew Jackson Downing, one of most prominent architects and landscape designers of the time, was struck by the numbers of people enjoying the outdoor pleasures of Green-Wood, which he described as "the largest and unquestionably the finest open space in the country." There were no public parks at the time, and he was convinced that New York City needed an open public space — "like Green-Wood except for the monuments . . . that would foster the love of rural beauty, and increase the knowledge of and taste for rare and beautiful trees and plants." Downing became one of the most vocal advocates for the creation of Central Park, and had he not tragically died in a steamboat accident in 1852, would surely have been its designer.

Preceding spread: View over the Gothic entrance gate designed by Richard Upjohn to the East River and Manhattan skyline.

Right: The canopy of a European horse-chestnut (*Aesculus hippocastanum*) shades monuments along Battle Avenue.

Left: European horse-chest-nut (*Aesculus hippocastanum*) in bloom.

Right: Cast-iron urns filled with Boston ferns mark the Burr family monument.

Today, Green-Wood, which now stretches across 478 acres, offers a peaceful oasis to visitors, as well as to its 570,000 permanent residents, many of them legendary names, such as Leonard Bernstein, Charles Ebbets, Jean-Michel Basquiat, Louis Comfort Tiffany, Horace Greeley, as well as many Civil War generals, baseball greats, politicians, artists, entertainers, and inventors. Even the infamous Boss Tweed, who died, disgraced, in Ludlow Street Jail, somehow managed to make it in, cleverly circumventing one of Green-Wood's early regulations that no one executed for a crime, or dying in jail, could be buried in its grounds.

There are more than 8,000 trees and shrubs at Green-Wood, which was recently accredited as a national arboretum. In 2012 Hurricane Sandy did enormous damage, felling almost 300 trees, and an extensive program of reforestation is underway. In collaboration with Cornell University, areas of lawn are being replaced with low-growing meadow grasses, which are drought tolerant and require little maintenance. In addition to pruning and tree work, a staff of six is responsible for planting 10,000 daffodils, tulips, snowdrops, and crocuses, maintaining 35 perennial beds, and handling the upkeep of five ponds, two of them glacial and three man-made.

These ponds are home to herons, egrets, geese, ducks, and sandpipers and there is always the chance of spotting an unusual migrant such as a pied-billed grebe, green-winged teal, hooded merganser, or American coot. Oak, European linden, maple, tulip sassafras, beech, chestnut, and even some elm trees attract warblers, tanagers, grosbeaks, and orioles, while fruit trees and berry bushes are magnets for fall migrants. There are red-tailed hawks and meadowlarks, owls, and even a colony of green and red monk parakeets (said to have escaped from a container that broke open at Idlewild [now Kennedy] Airport in the 1960s) who nest contentedly in the spires of the splendid gothic-arched main entrance at Fifth Avenue and 25th Street, designed by architect Richard Upjohn.

The historic importance of Green-Wood both for its architecture and its role as the forerunner of Central Park cannot be underestimated. But, now more than 150 years later, with a growing horticultural staff and the hindsight of the damage caused by Hurricane Sandy, there is a renewed emphasis on protecting and responsibly managing Green-Wood's natural environment for the enjoyment of future generations.

Above: Stewart family monument designed by Stanford White with bronze bas-reliefs by Augustus Saint-Gaudens.

Right: Entrance to the chapel designed by Warren & Wetmore in 1911.

Left: The fragrant mid-summer blooms of this allée of little-leaf linden *(Tilia cordata)* along Central Avenue are loved by bees and visitors.

Franklin D. Roosevelt Four Freedoms Park

Four Freedoms Park is perched on top of land-fill at the southern tip of Roosevelt Island. Its triangular site houses the timeless memorial to Roosevelt designed by legendary architect Louis I. Kahn. The memorial is set in a spare minimalist garden, and the perfect time to visit is a fall afternoon. Sunlight plays on the surface of the sloping granite walls that border each side of the magisterial flight of steps leading up to the memorial; a gentle breeze stirs the leaves of the two precisely aligned allées of linden trees; and there are incredible views of Manhattan's waterfront with glimpses of the Williamsburg and Brooklyn Bridges in the distance. Even the recently landmarked Pepsi Cola sign, across the water in Queens, seems imbued with extra levity.

When Kahn received the commission to design the memorial in 1973, the New York State Urban Development Corporation was planning to transform Welfare Island—a neglected sliver of land between midtown Manhattan and Queens—into an ambitious redevelopment site for middle-class housing. However, the memorial

Preceding spread: The bust of President Franklin Delano Roosevelt by Jo Davidson terminates the axis through the park.

Above: The embankments on the east and west sides of the memorial were hand-set on a steep 32-degree angle.

Opposite: The inscription of the Four Freedoms text was designed by Nicholas Benson of The John Stevens Shop in Newport, Rhode Island. Benson hand-carved the text on site.

IN THE FUTURE DAYS WHICH WE SEEK TO MAKE SECURE, WE LOOK FORWARD TO A WORLD FOUNDED UPON FOUR ESSENTIAL HUMAN FREEDOMS. THE FIRST IS FREEDOM OF SPEECH AND EXPRESSION - EVERYWHERE IN THE WORLD. THE SECOND IS FREEDOM OF EVERY PERSON TO WORSHIP GOD IN HIS OWN WAY - EVERYWHERE IN THE WORLD. THE THIRD IS FREEDOM FROM WANT... EVERYWHERE IN THE WORLD. THE FOURTH IS FREEDOM FROM FEAR... ANYWHERE IN THE WORLD. THAT IS NO VISION OF A DISTANT MILLENNIUM. IT IS A DEFINITE BASIS FOR A KIND OF WORLD ATTAINABLE IN OUR OWN TIME AND GENERATION.   FRANKLIN D. ROOSEVELT
JANUARY 6, 1941

was not finished until almost forty years later, and how this happened is something of a miracle.

The first disaster occurred in 1974 when Kahn died of a fatal heart attack in Penn Station shortly before the final schematic designs had been approved. His financially pressed office was closed, employees were let go, and Aldo Giurgola, his friend and colleague, moved the project to his New York office. The following year, New York City became enmeshed in a fiscal crisis so severe that it almost brought the city to bankruptcy, and all work on the memorial came to a stop.

Years went by and Kahn's posthumous project languished on the drawing books, seemingly doomed to oblivion. Then, in 2003, a fortuitous event, no-one could have foreseen, jump-started the project back to life. This was the release of the enormously popular film *My Architect: A Son's Journey* made by Kahn's son, Nathaniel, which sparked a huge interest in his father's work. This, in turn, led to an exhibition at Cooper Union of the design for the memorial and resulted in the formation of a small dedicated group determined to bring the project back to life. Led by William vanden Heuvel, they were able to raise $53 million from New York State, New York City, private foundations, and individuals. It was an incredible feat! Work began in 2010, and in 2012, the memorial was finally opened to the public.

Right: Monumental slabs of granite enclose The Room. Light filtering through the one-inch space between them mitigates the weight of the stone.

A garden had always been part of Kahn's plan. Harriet Pattison, the landscape architect in his office, who was also Nathaniel's mother, had primary responsibility for this aspect of the design and worked with him on revisions and changes. After Kahn's death, Lois Sherr Dubin was chosen by Giurgola's office as the landscape architect for the project but, since almost every aesthetic decision had already been made, her work was to come up with the best horticultural choices to meet the existing specifications.

The garden is stunningly simple in its conception. Five huge copper beeches, planted in a line and each set in a circular bed of pachysandra, form a boundary between the memorial and the ruins of a smallpox hospital, built in 1854 by James Renwick Jr., the architect of St. Patrick's Cathedral. Grown in Long Island, these beeches were 30-year-old specimens when they were planted, and are now 30 to 40 feet in height, forming a parallel line to the monumental steps, which ascend to the memorial. At the top of the steps, which are 100-feet wide, there is a tapered triangular lawn, flanked on either side by a double allée of 120 linden trees that direct the eye to a central focus point—a massive stone rising up from a stone piazza. The allées add drama and expectation, and hark back to the formal eighteenth-century gardens of Le Nôtre. They also focus our full attention on the huge granite block, in which a large niche holds an enlarged bronze version of the famous bust of Roosevelt by sculptor Jo Davidson. Suspended from the interior wall rather than sitting on a pedestal, the head appears to float in space. On the far side of the sculpture is The Room, open to the sky and enclosed on three sides by enormous slabs of granite that are almost but not quite joined. Here, one is invited to read the text of Roosevelt's famous "Four Freedoms" speech, to experience the spirit of great architecture, and to contemplate the spectacular view.

It would be hard to imagine this powerful and majestic monument without its softening landscape of trees and grass. Neither too much, nor too little, the lines and color of this minimalist garden are an integral part of the drama, humanizing the vastness of the granite, the brilliance of the detail, and the grandeur of the site. Kahn explains it best. "I had this thought," he said in 1973, speaking at a lecture he gave at Pratt shortly before he died, "that a memorial should be a room and a garden. That's all I had. Why did I want a room and a garden? I just chose it to be the point of departure. The garden is somehow a personal nature, a personal kind of control of nature, a gathering of nature. And the room was the beginning of architecture."

Native Plant Garden
New York Botanical Garden

Understanding a garden as a welcoming habitat for a large variety of interacting native flora is still a relatively new concept for many gardeners and garden lovers. The range and beauty of native plants is nowhere better demonstrated than at the Native Plant Garden at the New York Botanical Garden (NYBG), where almost 100,000 native trees, shrubs, wildflowers, ferns, and grasses are shown to great advantage in a contemporary-style garden that harmonizes with the natural landscape. Designed by landscape architect Sheila Brady of Oehme, van Sweden & Associates, with the help of a $15 million grant from the Leon Levy Foundation, the garden has close to 450 planted species, all native to the Northeast. Brady's design is spare and elegant, creating a sustainable, environmentally friendly garden with a strong modern sensibility, one that she wants people to see as "the real integration of ecology and site and design and horticulture."

Appropriately, the garden occupies the site of an earlier wildflower garden, created at the beginning of the twentieth century by Elizabeth Knight Britton, wife of NYBG's founding director, Nathaniel Lord Britton, and herself a serious botanist. It encompasses four distinct habitats: meadow, glades, woodlands, and wetlands. Many of the plants provide shelter and sustenance for wildlife, making this three-and-one-half acre garden a magnet for squirrels, chipmunks, frogs, and a colorful array of birds and butterflies.

The main focus of Brady's design is a series of three stepped geometric pools, where recycled rain water filtered by aquatic plants cascades down shallow stone weirs from pool to pool. The surrounding garden, framed by a forest of heritage oak trees that have been growing on the site since the nineteenth century, is planted with native trees, shrubs, ferns, grasses, and wildflowers. And for those who still harbor any doubts, it makes a compelling case that native plants can be as handsome as their more cultivated counterparts.

Visitors pass by a grid of symmetrically arranged sweetbay magnolias from Virginia at the main entrance of the garden to start on a route that takes them through a succession of shaded woodlands, dry open meadows, and lush wetlands. Their walk is sometimes on boardwalks made from native kiln-dried black locust, sometimes on paths that look like natural gravel but, in fact, are made up of tiny pebbles glued to a hard surface, and sometimes on mulch trails. The garden has been designed for year-round interest, and each section unfolds seamlessly into the next. It includes a diversity of growing conditions and features many different trees, shrubs, perennials, grasses, sedges, and wildflowers— all part of the great variety of plants native to northeast North America and all chosen here to take advantage of the varied natural landscape.

In spring, there are white trilliums, bloodroot, lady slipper orchids, Dutchman's breeches, and carpets of Virginia bluebells cover the woodland floor. In early summer, the air swarms with moths and butterflies amid swaths of mountain mint, golden rod, foam flowers, sunflowers, milk weed, and wild columbine. As summer progress, native asters and brilliant crimson-red lobelias hold sway to be followed by the russet red and purple

Preceding spread: Aquatic plants such as sweet flag are key components of an elaborate biofiltration system that helps reduce algal blooms.

Right: A gravel path leads to Split Rock, a massive Yonkers Gneiss glacial erratic that serves as a focal point in the meadow.

Overleaf: Water cascades over a weir constructed with a seven-ton slab of dark Hamilton bluestone quarried in the Catskills near Albany, New York.

hues of meadow grasses and a heady foliage of maples, blackgums, tulip trees, red-stemmed dogwoods, and river birches. Winter is the time to see clusters of red winterberry fruit and to take in the architecture of the bare trees, sharply rising above huge natural rock outcroppings.

This garden not only shows the beauty of native flora throughout the seasons but also demonstrates how native plants, chosen for their visual impact, sustainability, and adaptability, can offer environmental benefits, such as filtering water and air, preventing erosion, and providing shelter for wildlife. Locally sourced and recycled materials are used throughout the garden. Benches are made of salvaged and recycled wood; the pools are fed by rainwater captured and recycled on site and regulated by an underground cistern; and air is pumped into the water to keep it moving and to prevent the pools from freezing solid in winter.

"A garden like this is all about process and transformation," explains Michael Hagen, the garden's curator. "We have a mandate," he says, "to monitor how plants respond to climate change. We watch the meadow carefully to maintain a balance, and if a plant is not sustainable, we try something else. In short, we're working it out as we go along." Hagen is correct. Nothing is static or fixed. Plants and garden are a work in progress, and this is what makes the Native Plant Garden a vastly enjoyable learning experience in every season.

Left: Cardinal flower, ostrich fern, sedges, and other moisture-tolerant native plants soften the black locust boardwalk that runs the length of the pools.

Left: In summer, bright-yellow goldenrod and white flowering spurge provide sweeps of color amid the grasses of the dry meadow.

Conservatory Garden
Central Park

The name is a little misleading since there is no conservatory in what is the most beautiful garden in Central Park. The garden takes its name from the the elegant glass greenhouse complex that stood on this site at the end of the nineteenth century. More than a dozen gardeners nurtured tropical plants for public display and supplied plants for all New York City's parks.

The greenhouses were a popular destination, and records show that in 1900 more than 600,000 visitors came to see the displays. In later years, the expense of heating and maintaining the glass buildings became prohibitive, and they fell into disrepair. At the height of the Depression in 1934, Robert Moses, then parks commissioner, made the decision to replace them with a formal garden. It was a WPA project with Gilmore Clarke of the Parks Department serving as the consulting landscape architect and the delightfully named M. Betty Sprout, also a landscape architect, in charge of the planting scheme.

On September 19, 1937, the new six-acre garden opened with great fanfare. Its main entrance was through the magnificent wrought-iron Vanderbilt Gate on Fifth Avenue between 104th and 105th Streets. From here, visitors approached not one but three separate gardens, each with a distinct style— French, Italian, and English. Reporting on the event, the *New York Times* commented, "Thousands of hardy perennials, leafy shrubs, climbing vines, and countless varieties of red, yellow, blue and purple flowers are planted in symmetric designs. A contrast is offered to the screeching of brakes and roaring of engines as the endless stream of automobiles passes within sight of Fifth Avenue."

By the early 1970s, Central Park had become a virtual wasteland, and the north end was perceived as one of the most dangerous areas. Fortuitously, help arrived, first from the New York Committee of the Garden Club of America, and then in the early 1980s from the newly formed Central Park Conservancy. A private nonprofit organization born out of community concern, the conservancy was created to restore and maintain Central Park under a contract with the city. Elizabeth Barlow Rogers, an urban planner and landscape historian, was its first president, and she persuaded garden designer Lynden Miller to undertake the restoration of the Conservatory Garden.

There was no budget, and Miller did all her own fundraising while beginning work on the redesign of the garden. While committed to the layout of the existing garden, Miller was not convinced by Betty Sprout's choice of perennials, which she felt were very high maintenance and emphasized bloom over foliage. Miller came up with new plan that combined ornamental shrubs and large groupings of perennials in five large mixed borders and seasonal plantings in smaller inner beds.

Today, the Vanderbilt Gate brings visitors into the Italianate garden, with its imposing rectangular lawn, ringed at the far end with alternating yew and

Preceding spread and right: The broad arc of a pergola draped with wisteria completes the axis of the central Italianate garden.

Above and opposite: Double
allées of crab apple trees
flank the paths on either side
of the central lawn.

Left: The Burnett Memorial Fountain by Bessie Potter Vonoh animates the lily pond in the south garden.

Above: Summer annuals include bronze fennel, Salvia farinacea, and coleus 'Sedona.'

spirea tiered hedges and flanked on either side by double crabapple allées. Across the lawn, a single jet fountain is framed by a wisteria-covered pergola. To the left is the south (English) garden, with three concentric horseshoe-shaped rings of beds. In the outer ring, euonymous hedging encloses French lilac. The center ring beds, redesigned by Miller in 1983, are mixed borders of trees, shrubs, grasses, and perennials. The innermost ring, with serpentine hedges of Japanese holly, is designed annually by Diane Schaub, director of the garden, with spring bulbs followed by dozens of annuals in displays that play off the perennial beds across the bluestone paths.

The north garden (to the right of the Italianate garden) is French in style, featuring small parterre beds arranged around a bronze fountain (*Three Dancing Maidens* by Walter Schott, 1910.) A second tier of larger beds encircles the parterre arrangement. Each spring the beds are a dazzling display of 20,000

tulips and in the fall, 2,000 Korean chrysanthemums take their place. White flowering spirea and ever-blooming roses are planted on the next terraced level, where pergolas are covered with luminous white climbing Silver Moon roses that arch over the curving paths.

Considered by many to be the most beautiful historic garden in the city, the Conservatory Garden is an illustrious example of intelligent garden restoration, one where structure has been respected but plantings continue to evolve. Under Schaub's direction, the original yew hedge design has been recreated and

Above and opposite: A rich tapestry of of spring bulbs in the south garden contrasts with the sweep of tulips in the parterre beds that surround the fountain in the north garden.

hundreds of other shrubs, perennials, and trees have been added to beds and woodland areas within the garden.

As visitors pass through the imposing entrance gate, few are aware of the garden's fractured past, let alone its miraculous resurrection. For them, it's a beautiful garden, and thanks to a permanent endowment from the Weiler-Arnow family for maintenance, its future is secure.

Abby Aldrich Rockefeller Sculpture Garden
Museum of Modern Art

The earliest MoMA garden on West 54th Street was planned by Alfred H. Barr Jr., the museum's first director, and John McAndrew, curator of architecture. A row of brownstones behind the original 1939 building designed by Philip Goodwin and Edward Durrell Stone was demolished shortly before the museum opened, and a very simple garden was hastily created to fill the space.

Experiencing sculpture in an outdoor setting was something entirely new at the time, and MoMA's gallery in a garden was an immediate success—so much so that by the late 1940s, when David Rockefeller took over as MoMA's president, the museum decided it needed something more permanent. Philip Johnson was commissioned to undertake a complete redesign of the space and landscape architect James Fanning was hired to take charge of the plantings.

The new garden, named in honor of Rockefeller's mother, opened in April 1953. In an interview with *The New Yorker*, Johnson referred to the former garden as "just a collection of trees," adding "We all felt there were ways of showing sculpture to better advantage than in a back yard." He recounted that he had "always loved St. Mark's Square in Venice," and that his idea was to create a piazza, which he described as "a sort of outdoor room. A roofless room with four sub-rooms, formed by the planting and the canals to provide four space backgrounds for the sculpture."

Johnson's design was spare and elegant, and his decision to make the garden on two levels was brilliant. The western upper platform was a dining terrace shaded by a line of hornbeams; the lower terrace was sunk two feet below grade and intersected by two canals, each spanned by a bridge. The entire courtyard was paved with long, rectilinear slabs of Vermont marble. Two plane trees were kept from the earlier incarnation, and cryptomeria and birch trees were introduced to help break up the space and to control the placement and visibility of the sculpture. A fourteen-foot gray-brick wall with a gate and a grille was built along the 54th Street side. This was done because, as Johnson explained, "It gives emotional release from the inside and keeps the street passerby from feeling excluded."

In the same *New Yorker* interview, published three days before the opening of the garden, Fanning talks about using pachysandra, creeping roses, and myrtle and winter jasmine as ground cover, but he does not mention the ivy that has been associated with the garden for so many decades.

Again in 1964, under Johnson's aegis, the garden was enlarged and this seems to have been the moment when ivy became the permanent ground cover throughout the garden. A Lombardy poplar tree was added to screen an office building on the east side of the garden and the cryptomerias were replaced with weeping beeches. Additional birch trees were also added by landscape architects Zion and Breen, the same firm that handled the garden's further restoration following the museum's expansion between 2000 and 2004 by Yoshio Taniguchi.

Preceding spread and left: Two pools, separated by a stand of weeping beeches define the space. At the head of the smaller pool is *The River* by Aristide Maillol. Henri Matisse's four-panel *Back* is installed on the wall.

Left: Seen from the second floor of the museum, the precise geometry of the design is revealed.

At that time, the east and west terraces were expanded, the marble paving was replaced with a lighter Georgia marble, and the brick wall was replaced by a solid aluminum screen that cuts off the museum from the street and has little aesthetic appeal. The garden is now elevated on three sides but the central area is still sunken. From inside the museum, the garden is visible through a huge glass facade, and this allows it to be experienced as a continuation of the indoor space.

In spite of changes made over the years, the core of Johnson's modernist design remains intact. For almost seven decades, this Midtown oasis—with its striated marble paving, pools of water, jagged angular beds, small groves of delicate birch trees, and large expanse of ivy has showcased masterpieces of the museum's sculpture collection. Among those works inextricably linked with MoMA's garden are Gaston Lachaise's *Standing Woman* (1932) and Maillol's *The River* (1938–40), a massive reclining body of a woman who seems to be in danger of falling into the water. The garden has also been the site of many temporary shows including an exhibition house by Marcel Breuer (1949) and a traditional Japanese house and garden (1954.)

In 2004 MoMA announced a controversial plan to allow free access from the street at all times to the public. Although the plan was later dropped, the outcry it provoked revealed how intensely people on both sides of the issue cared about the garden. Landscape architect Michael Van Valkenburgh stated it best: "What is so brilliant about the garden and what makes it great [is] this cloistered isolation."

Left: Clusters of birch trees are set in beds of ivy, each with its own distinctive and unusual cut-out shape.

New York Chinese Scholar's Garden
Staten Island

That New York City has an authentic classical Chinese garden on Staten Island is largely result of one woman's vision, energy, and determination. In 1982, when Frances X. Paulo Huber became executive director of the Staten Island Botanical Garden (later to become part of Snug Harbor Cultural Center), it was not in good shape. The gardens, buildings, walkways, and roadways were in disrepair. There were weeds everywhere, the greenhouse had no glass, and the trees—American chestnuts, black pines, silver maples, and Norway maples—needed pruning.

Huber was asked by the trustees to come up with a master plan. Trained as a landscape architect at the University of Massachusetts at Amherst, she decided that a new focus was needed and that it should be a classical Chinese scholar's garden. Her goal, she explains, was to emphasize China's importance in the history of horticulture and to link to the heritage of Staten Island residents who had been engaged in the China Sea trade. As she recalls, "Most people thought I was crazy and no one was very encouraging, but I was not deterred."

Classical Chinese gardens seek to recreate natural landscapes in miniature and to reflect the metaphysical importance of natural beauty in their design. From antiquity, gardens have played an important role in the cultural life of China. The Tang dynasty (618–907 AD) is considered to have been the first golden age of the classical Chinese garden. During the Mongol invasion of China in the thirteenth century, many scholars, who were part of China's elite, fled to Suzhou, where they created exquisite gardens.

Suzhou is a city of bridges, canals, and rivers near the northern shore of Lake Tai. To Marco Polo, it was the "Venice of the Orient." Today, it is a UNESCO World Heritage Site and its Humble Administrator's Garden and Lingering Garden are considered to be two of the four most famous classical gardens in China. Suzhou was where Huber turned to find craftsmen with the skills to make her garden a reality. With the help of the Metropolitan Museum of Art, which had recently completed its Astor Chinese Garden Court, she got in touch with the Landscape Architecture Company of China and met Zou Gongwu, China's leading scholar of classical garden design, whom she hired as chief designer for her proposed garden.

Huber made four trips to China to study and learn more about classical gardens. Working with the Landscape Architecture Company, she was able interest the Chinese government in the project, and they agreed to pay for the labor and a portion of the materials. The work would be done in Suzhou, with the cost of shipping the materials to Staten Island and the construction of the garden to be paid by city and state funds, and grants from the National Endowment for the Arts, private foundations, and individual donors.

In 1998 a team of forty Chinese artists and artisans, along with their own chef, arrived from Suzhou to assemble the garden. Construction took six months, and the following year this extraordinary garden was opened to the public.

Preceding spread: Japanese maples and lace bark pine frame a view of the Knowing Fish Pavilion with the garden entrance beyond.

Right: In the inner courtyard, the Pavilion of Chilly Green opens to the One-Step Bridge. Japanese maple, Chinese plum, and a peach tree are planted in front of the walls.

Left: Flowering dogwood and winter jasmine in the outer courtyard between the Moon Gate and the Bridge of Flowing Purity.

A classical scholar's garden is designed according to strict rules. The entrance is a narrow passageway that serves as a place of meditation before visitors arrive in the garden proper. A white wall, intended to provide a stark contrast to the natural colors of the plants and trees, encloses the garden, which contains decorative rocks, pavilions, and bridges. Water is a key element, and within the courtyard there is an inner garden structured around a pond. Borrowed views are an important design element, and a juxtaposition of varying shapes, colors, and textures is intended to create a sense of infinite space within an enclosed area.

All these elements are to be found in the New York Chinese Scholar's Garden, which contains three courtyards, a teahouse, three bridges, five pavilions, three ponds, a waterfall, and a stream. A series of walls, pavilions, and corridors emanate from the main courtyard, offering glimpses of other rooms and garden vignettes. The heavily eroded rocks from Lake Tai jut out of the largest pond while a smaller pond is visible from a moon gate.

At first, this garden seems to be primarily about rocks, buildings, and pathways, but plants are an equally important part of the design, and they have been carefully chosen for their shape, color, bloom time, fragrance, and symbolic meaning. There are more than eighty species growing in this garden, including rhododendrons, peonies, magnolias, Japanese maples, pines, bamboo, flowering apricots, plum, and wintersweet.

Visitors who remember to leave their Western minds at the gate will find themselves in another world and be well rewarded. Frances Huber deserves our gratitude for this singular garden. Making it happen was a remarkable achievement and the garden now engages thousands of students of Chinese heritage and culture through seasonal festivals and meditation practice. Now almost twenty years old, the garden is very much in need of restoration, and a move is getting underway to raise the funds. Not surprisingly, Huber, now retired, still plans to be involved.

Above: The Weeping Willow
Window in the Knowing
Fish Pavilion. Flying eaves,
designed to give the sense
that the roof is floating,
frame the view of the sky.

Opposite: View from
the Passage of Tranquility
across to the Weeping
Willow Window and
the scarlet leaves of the
Japanese maple.

Far left: River birches set against a backdrop of lace bark pine.

Left: Bamboo Path leading to the garden.

Paley Park
Manhattan

Tucked between two buildings on 53rd Street just east of Fifth Avenue, Paley Park (its official name is Samuel Paley Plaza but no one ever seems to call it that) is an enduring example of good civic garden design. It opened in 1967, commissioned by William Paley, the former chairman of CBS, as a memorial to his father. He was closely involved in its creation, selecting landscape architect Robert L. Zion to design the park in a small space created by the demolition of a townhouse once occupied by the fabled Stork Club.

Urban reformer Jacob Riis is credited with inventing the concept of a pocket-park in 1897, but his idea did not catch on until after World War II, when bombed-out building sites in European cities provided the opportunity to create small parks. In this country, no one paid much attention to the notion until 1966 when Thomas Hoving, then the city parks commissioner, identified 378 vacant lots and 346 abandoned buildings in Bedford-Stuyvesant alone, and encouraged making some of them into small parks.

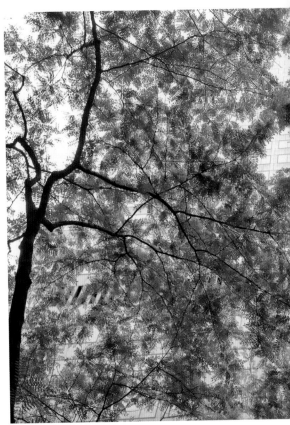

A few years earlier, Zion, a former vice president of the Architectural League, had also been thinking about the subject, and in 1963 he displayed a series of plans for vest-pocket parks at an exhibition that was organized by the League. When Paley decided to make a park on his small Midtown site, Zion was his obvious choice as designer.

Paley Park was an immediate success, quickly becoming the prototype for a new kind of public space—a small, privately maintained mid-block refuge from the rigors of the city. Bounded by buildings on three sides, the park is set back and slightly elevated, separated from the street by three shallow steps. The entire site is the shape of shoe box and no more than one-tenth of an acre. It is dominated by a twenty-foot high waterfall that cascades down the rear wall. This sheet of water is not only the key aesthetic feature of the garden but the noise it makes serves a highly practical purpose in drowning out the sound of nearby street traffic.

Left: Rushing water from the waterfall effectively drowns out the noise of Midtown traffic.

Center: Well-placed honey locust trees provide dappled shade and ambience.

Opposite: Three steps leading to the water backdrop add drama and definition. Raising the garden above the sidewalk increases the sense of place.

Two high sidewalls frame the garden and are planted with ivy to give the effect of what Zion called a "vertical lawn." Seventeen honey locust trees, planted on a grid in the central seating area, offer a shaded green canopy over a floor of rough granite pavers, home to the lightweight white wire frames of Harry Bertoia's classic mesh chairs. The neutral palette of gray, green, and white is accentuated by container plantings of colorful if conventional annuals. At night, the ornamental iron entrance gate is closed, limiting access but still allowing the park and its dramatic back-lit waterfall to be seen from the street.

This jewel of a garden is a welcome escape from the ceaseless noise and endless motion of its Midtown surroundings. Its design is simple and brilliant with the sound and sight of water always present. As fresh today as when it opened more than fifty years ago, Paley Park is an exemplary modernist solution for transforming a vacant lot into a serene and beautiful urban space.

Heather Garden

Fort Tryon Park

The Heather Garden is one of the hidden treasures of New York City. This three-acre garden, perched high on a ridge more than two hundred feet above the Hudson River at the southern end of Fort Tryon Park, has unparalleled views of the river, and is within walking distance of the Cloisters. Now a city, state, and federal landmark, its provenance is superb. Frederick Law Olmsted Jr. and his stepbrother, John Charles Olmsted, were commissioned to create the garden by John D. Rockefeller in 1935, before he gave Fort Tryon Park to the city.

Planned as a series of west-facing terraces that cut into the steep hillside and emanate from a formal promenade, the garden is composed two wave-shaped mixed borders bisected by a central pathway. One is filled with shrubs, perennials, and bulbs while the other contains a carefully curated collection of heaths and heathers with companion plantings. A terrace of linden trees, through which visitors can snatch dramatic glimpses of the Hudson, separates the garden from the rugged lanscape below.

It is hard to believe that when Fort Tryon Park was created, the land was barren and windswept with massive rocky protrusions and precipitous escarpments. Emphasizing this contrast between wild and cultivated was very much part of Olmsted's original plan. He wanted visitors to have a "sense of the luminous space beyond and below the foliage," and his design specified "a gardenesque area of heaths and heathers which thrive in open barren areas and whose low height would preserve views of the Hudson River."

Like many of the city's gardens, this one fell into precipitous decline during the fiscal crisis of the 1970s. But in 1983, the Greenacre Foundation stepped in to fund a restoration plan to bring the garden back to life. The work was undertaken by the New York City Parks Department and Quennell Rothschild & Partners, a landscape architecture firm that worked closely with horticulturist Timothy Steinhoff. A conservancy group was established to help raise funds, and in 2009 the garden received another boost when public-garden designers Lynden Miller and Ronda Brands were commissioned by the Fort Tryon Park Trust Consevancy to reinvigorate the planting and to come up with a solution that would respect the spirit of the original design but provide more year-round interest.

Today, the Heather Garden is home to 550 varieties of flowering trees, shrubs, and perennials. Working with the Northeast Heather Society, the park's designers and gardeners have carefully selected dozens of heaths and heathers that offer a sweep of changing colors and textures in every season. Both heaths and heathers are evergreens, with green, yellow, or red foliage that can turn silver, copper, or even chocolate brown during winter months. Heaths (*Erica* species and cultivars) usually flower from mid-winter to early spring, and these are followed by heathers (*Calluna vulgaris* cultivars) that begin in mid-summer. In spring, crocus, snowdrops, hellebores, and daffodils give way to drifts of Spanish bluebells, catmint, Siberian iris, tulips, soon to be followed by rhododendrons, azaleas, peonies, dogwoods, and flowering quince. Summer brings musk roses, hibiscus, clematis, and hydrangeas, while the fall foliage of asters, Japanese anemones, and sages offers continuing drama. During the winter months, the heaths transform the heather bed into an undulating sweep of pinks and whites.

Preceding spread: The heather bed in summer.

Right: In late winter, swaths of heaths and heathers welcome visitors with their pink, white, and magenta flowers and evergreen, chocolate, gold, and lime foliage.

Above and opposite:
'Aquilegia 'Yellow Queen',
Ornamental Allium, and
azalea are among the multi-
tude of flowering plants that
bloom in early spring.

Opposite and above: In autumn, textures abound. The Franklinia's copper foliage is a beautiful contrast to Solomon Seal (*Polygonatum*), *Verbena bonariensis*, Stachys (Lambs Ears) and the deep purple of the Aster "October Skies" that drape the base of a Siberian Elm.

World Trade Center Memorial Garden

A minimalist garden of trees on a flat open plaza surrounds the 9/11 Memorial designed by Israeli-American architect Michael Arad with landscape architect Peter Walker. Visitors approach the two reflecting pools that occupy the footprint of the Twin Towers through a glade of four hundred swamp white oaks. These are placed in rigid formation on symmetrical strips of grass—not welcoming but reassuring as the scale is human and in contrast to the overwhelming sight and sound of the gigantic pools.

Conceived by Arad as "voids that will never fill," the pools are each nearly an acre in size. Their giddying depth is mesmerizing, and the sound of the water drowns out all others. After viewing the victims' names inscribed on the bronze parapets of the voids, visitors fall away, moving back through the garden to take a measure of comfort from the lines of trees. They appear to be planted in the ground but in fact they are set on a green roof that covers the structure that houses the Memorial Museum.

It is an utterly simple garden, an arrangement of trees, granite benches, pavers, cobblestones, and grass beds. The shadows in the joints between the pavers and the cobbles create a subtle banding pattern that breaks the vast plane of the Memorial into a human-sized space. With time, the white oaks, all grown in New Jersey, promise to grow into a cathedral of arching branches.

One tree stands apart from all the others. It is a Callery pear tree that was discovered in the rubble a month after 9/11 at Ground Zero, severely damaged with snapped roots and burned and broken branches. To the untrained eye, the tree looked dead but it was taken to a Parks Department nursery in the Bronx, where it was nursed back to life and cared for by horticulturist Richie Cabo. Returned to the 9/11 Memorial site in 2010, the tree was planted in a prominent spot near the South Pool. Known as the Survivor tree, its short-lived but prolific spring blooms signify hope and rebirth.

Preceding spread: The monumental waterfalls create an atmosphere for private contemplation and a sense of the infinite.

Left and right: Simple granite blocks serve as benches and are set on granite cobblestones. These intersect with larger pavers placed within the symmetrical grid of grass and trees.

Left: In the distance is 1 World Trade Center, the main building of the rebuilt World Trade Center complex.

Above: The Callery pear tree that was found in the rubble of 9/11, nursed back to health, and returned the site. Its bloom time is brief but beautiful.

Enid A. Haupt Conservatory

New York Botanical Garden

The Enid A. Haupt Conservatory is a superb example of a late Victorian-style glasshouse, an architectural treasure, and a New York City landmark. It is the focal point of NYBG and a garden of high theatrical drama, serving as the venue for shows with blockbuster production values, exotic stars, unusual cameo appearances, and often a cast of thousands (plants not people).

The building is made up of eleven pavilions that extend from a central space rising ninety feet to a spectacular dome. Modeled after the palm house at Kew Gardens and Joseph Paxton's Crystal Palace at the London Exposition of 1851, the conservatory was designed by Lord and Burnham, the preeminent glasshouse company of its day. Groundbreaking took place on January 3, 1899, and the conservatory was completed three years later. The building is named in honor of philanthropist Enid Annenberg Haupt, whose extraordinary generosity saved it from demolition in 1978 and continues to support its maintenance.

In addition to its permanent collection of palms, cycads, and plant collections from the tropical rain forests and the deserts of Africa and America, the conservatory serves as the backdrop for three or four special exhibitions each year. The Orchid Show is held from January to the beginning of April, and showcases more than 8,000 seductive and exotic orchids (so many, in fact, that no one ever does an actual head count). It's a large-scale production, and should a cast member begin to droop, there are any number of understudies eagerly waiting in the wings and ready to step on stage. About half the orchids are grown in NYBG's own greenhouses (the number increases every year) and the remainder are purchased from dealers and growers to be shipped to the garden in heated trucks.

Each year there is a different theme, but whatever the focus, there is always an astonishing diversity of orchid species on show. Eye-dazzling displays of epiphytes, cattleyas, miltoniopsis, psychopsis, vanilla orchids, vandas, paphiopedilums, onicidiums, phaleaenopsis, cymbidiums, and other species are a tour de force of color, shape, and size. They tumble, overflow, and vie for attention, making visitors believe, despite the cold and snow outside, that this opulent orchid garden is their natural habitat.

May brings a summer spectacular that more often than not is a double-header. It's a winning formula whereby visitors can view a selection of works in the gallery or displayed outside by the artists, humanists, or landscape designers whose work has inspired the horticultural display that takes place within the conservatory. This has included the glassworks of Dale Chihuly, Beatrix Farrand's garden for the Rockefellers on Mount Desert, a rendering of Charles Darwin's English garden, and a recreation of Frida Kahlo's studio and garden at Casa Azul.

The behind-the-scenes preparations for these shows involves many staff, intense planning, and intricate staging. Each one is meticulously researched by the garden's curatorial and horticultural staff and, as with the orchids, the plants used within the glasshouse have been carefully propagated to bloom sequentially so that when a flower withers or fades, it gets whisked away to be

Preceding spread: Weeping Japanese flowering cherries planted in honor of long-serving NYBG Trustee Beth Straus line the front of the Conservatory.

Right: The Orchid Show, held in late winter since 2002, serves as a welcome prelude to spring.

discreetly replaced by another glorious specimen. Protected from the vagaries of drafts, winds, and pests, these imaginary gardens, which appear so precise and lifelike, are all delicious artifice.

"Kiku: The Art of the Japanese Chrysanthemum" is another kind of artifice that takes place most years in early October. Kiku is a floral tradition at least 1,500 years old, where chrysanthemum blossoms are grown from seed and trained to flower in highly elaborate floral arrangements. These can be in the shape of bridges, cascades, and the show-stopping ozukori dome, which features hundred of blooms grown from one stem and strung through individual wire holders that are part of a massive wired armature. The cultivation and training of one plant takes at least twelve months and the meticulous preparation and design skills needed for this exhibit are astonishing.

The final extravaganza of the year is the Holiday Train Show in which G-scale model trains zip through replicas of New York landmarks, each crafted out of natural materials such as bark, twigs, stems, fruits, seeds, and pine cones. Each year more buildings are added; there are now 149 structures, including Hudson River mansions, the old Yankee Stadium, and the Rose Center for Earth and Space, its interior sphere made of dried rose petals.

Gardens, even the most naturalistic, take maintenance and care. But nothing compares to the patience, expertise, and production skills exercised by the team of talented gardeners who work at the Enid A. Haupt Conservatory. Under the leadership of curator Francisca Coelho, they have raised the art of plant showmanship to dazzling heights, making new magic every year.

Left: Since 2007 NYBG horticulturists have grown, trained, and displayed chrysanthemums using ancient techniques perfected by Japanese Kiku masters at Shinjuku Gyoen National Garden in Tokyo.

Above and opposite: Using elaborate set pieces and sophisticated plantings, NYBG gardeners completely transform the conservatory several times each year. This horticultural stagecraft has evoked settings ranging from Frida Kahlo's Mexico City courtyard garden to the lush rain forests of Asia and South America.

Left: For *Impressionism: American Gardens on Canvas* in 2016, NYBG horticulturists created borders of forced annuals and perennials to capture the spirt of poet Celia Thaxter's cottage garden on Appledore Island in Maine.

Carl Schurz Park

Manhattan

"If this park was a guy, I'd be in love with him," reads the blog of a recent visitor to Carl Schurz Park in Yorkville on the Upper East Side. It's fair to say she would not have felt this way had she been there forty years ago when the park was dangerous, deserted, and run down—a victim of the economic woes of the 1970s. But, thanks to the efforts of local residents, the park and its gardens have since been saved, and this is a story that ends well.

Before the Revolution, Yorkville was farmland. By the early nineteenth century, reachable only by boat from Lower Manhattan, it had become a desirable escape for New York's merchant elite. However, by the end of the century with the opening of the Second and Third Avenue Els, Yorkville became a middle-to-working-class neighborhood and home to immigrants from Germany, Poland, Hungary, and Ireland.

The city acquired a small parcel of land in 1876 to be used as a park, adding an additional two parcels over the next twenty years. In 1902

a landscape design by Calvert Vaux and Samuel Parsons Jr. for paths, iron railings, and a solid seawall was completed. Originally called East River Park, its name was changed eight years later when the German-American residents of Yorkville petitioned to rename it in honor of Carl Schurz, the first German-American to be elected to the Senate and Secretary of the Interior under President Rutherford B. Hayes. The construction of the FDR Drive in the 1940s led to the park's expansion and redesign, and it now runs from East End Avenue to the water between East 84th and East 90th Streets.

By the early 1970s, the park had become unsafe, dangerous, and dilapidated, being described by the *New York Times* as "a wasteland of eroded hillsides and burned turf." In 1974 a group of concerned residents formed the Carl Schurz Community Association, and two years later the first-ever restoration of a city park planned and funded by a community group got underway. Working in conjunction with the Parks Department, the association installed a new drainage system and replaced several dead cherry trees. A further renovation was completed in 1992, and the association, now called the Carl Schurz Park Conservancy, has been working ever since in partnership with the city to improve and maintain the park. The city pays for one gardener and the Conservancy funds another plus two seasonal helpers.

Preceding spread: The path from the 87th Street entrance leads to Peter Pan Circle.

Above and right: Planting along the Esplanade overlooking the East River.

Overleaf: One of two grand staircases that ascend to the upper level garden from the main entrance at 86th Street.

However, it is the large and dedicated corps of volunteers who are the key to the health and vigor of the gardens. They actively fundraise, handle seasonal clean-ups, and take responsibility for the planting of individual beds.

An allée of cherry trees at the 86th Street entrance to the park leads to a dramatically sloped semi-circular planting bed positioned between two grand staircases. These ascend to the upper area of the garden where more flowerbeds are recessed into the back of a long promenade facing the East River. On either side of the lower garden, a network of winding paths and stone walls connects to various other parts of the garden, which include open lawns, a children's playground, and two dog runs. A favorite corner and one beloved by generations of children is home to a bronze statue of Peter Pan— his attention focused on a fawn, a rabbit, and a frog grouped around his feet. Charles Andrew Hafner created the sculpture in 1928 as part of a fountain for the lobby of the former Paramount theatre on 42nd Street. It was donated to the park in 1975, where it was placed in a circular bed, edged with a stone wall. In 1998 the statue was stolen and, amazingly, recovered by the police from the East River, where someone had seen it being thrown by a group of teenage thieves.

Back on his pedestal, Peter Pan is surrounded by a mass of tulips in the spring, a variety of annuals in the summer, and chrysanthemums in the fall. The planting and care of this flowerbed are the responsibility of a volunteer gardener. She plans the design, chooses the colors—they need to be uniform and bright and light enough to be seen in the distance—and worries about the watering. That Peter Pan and his flowerbed are so well looked after is indicative of the energy and dedication of the volunteer members of the Carl Schurz Park Conservancy. Their efforts have transformed this once languishing desolate and dangerous place into a model urban green space, now a draw for the surrounding community.

Right: Peter Pan Circle.

Brooklyn Bridge Park

Brooklyn Bridge Park is one of New York's most ambitious new parks. It spans eighty-five acres of the East River waterfront in the Brooklyn Heights and Dumbo neighborhoods, extending in a long, narrow stretch of land from Jay Street to Atlantic Avenue and jutting out on four piers (2,3,5,6) into the river. A fifth pier (1) is a large rectangle built on landfill, and what remains of pier 4 has been planted with trees to make a tiny island and bird sanctuary.

For the longest time, New York seemed resolutely turned inward as if almost willfully forgetting that four of its five boroughs are islands. Brooklyn residents could walk on the Brooklyn Heights promenade and take in spectacular views of Manhattan, but they were entirely cut off from the waterfront by the Brooklyn Queens Expressway. The park site, formerly an industrial shipping and storage complex built by the Port Authority of New York and New Jersey in the 1950s, became obsolete when container shipping was introduced. Brooklyn Bridge Park has not only transformed a significant stretch of post-industrial waterfront into a thriving urban landscape but Brooklynites are now intimately connected to their shoreline, with direct access from a pedestrian bridge.

Not surprisingly, the process of making the park has been torturously long and drawn out with many travails. It is hard to believe that ground was broken by Mayor Rudolph Giuliani on July 26, 2001. Three years later, Michael Van Valkenburgh, who came on as a consultant in 1998, was hired as the landscape architect for the project. He and his firm are still at work since some parts of the park are still under construction.

In 1999 a community meeting was held to find out what local residents would like to see in a park. An elderly woman, Mary Ellen Murphy, stood up and announced that since she lived on a small fixed income and could not escape the summer heat, she wanted to be able to walk on grass at dusk, take off her shoes, and stand in the East River while gazing at the stars and seeing the reflection of the moon. Her wish became Van Valkenburgh's mantra. In his words: "It was one of those paradigm shifts in park-making history, where we realized that this park wasn't about scenery. The nature of this park is the river."

The park follows the river for almost a mile, and ornamental plantings and woodland areas are interspersed throughout the sports fields, ball courts, roller skating rink, sandy beach, a restored 1922 carousel, bicycle paths, and large open lawns ideal for picnicking and performing arts events. The two main garden areas, however, are to be found on piers 1 and 6, at either end of the park. These gardens are not only beautiful, but they also offer shade, block wind, and provide habitats for birds, butterflies, and bees, and all are managed organically with water recirculated for irrigation.

Creating a garden on Pier 1 presented special problems. It was a virtually treeless site and the only pier to be constructed on a landfill rather than on piles. The challenge was not only to plant trees and shrubs but also to make the space feel more interesting. Van Valkenburgh's solution was to raise

Preceding spread: The east pier of Brooklyn Bridge provides a backdrop to a stormwater treatment wetland edged with Joe Pye weed, Culvers root, bulrush, willow, and shadbush.

Right: A rip-rap wall (constructed of large boulders), a remnant pile field, a pitch pine, the Pier 1 salt marsh, and the Manhattan skyline create a diversely textured view from within the park.

Left: A dense planting of swamp milkweed and ox eye sunflowers contributes to the multisensory experience of Pier 6.

the ground by thirty feet and construct a series of mounds and hills. All of the soil was imported and this garden, which looks so natural, is, in fact, entirely artificial. A series of winding paths now crisscross the area, making an intimate landscape between the groves of London plane, honey locust, Kentucky coffee bean, catalpa, and pin oaks, all selected because they do well near water and can stand up to wind. In spring, a sumac path is carpeted with wildflowers, and close to the river there is a salt marsh filled with grasses and granite boulders. Five ponds, each with different ornamental plantings, are connected by four weirs that allow the water to flow between them, making a secluded enclave where city dwellers can see butterflies, watch birds, and savor nature.

Pier 6, once a five-acre concrete span, now incorporates a beautiful wild garden. It is filled with hundreds of native species from sedges to rushes to flowers to ferns. Having numerous species of blooming flowers as well as milkweed attracts large populations of bees and monarch butterflies. The farthest edge of the pier is home to a flower field. This is a half-acre span of neatly cut grass that features multiple patches of dense native wildflowers which bloom from spring until late fall.

The park offers a panorama of the Manhattan skyline, bounded on the north by the Brooklyn Bridge and on the south by the Statue of Liberty. Its design includes a variety of salvaged materials: wooden pilings from the old piers remain in place, salvaged granite blocks create banks of seating, and the wood for benches comes from the yellow pine timbers of a demolished warehouse on the site. Sustainability has been applied across a range of spheres—ecological, structural, cultural, and economic. Guided by the concept of "post-industrial nature," the design uses unabashedly man-made landscapes to kick-start new site ecologies.

By creating a man-made landscape that thrives in a heavily used urban setting, Van Valkenburgh and Matthew Urbanski, the lead architect for the project, have designed a park able to absorb crowds that sometimes exceed

300,000 visitors on a summer weekend. No mean feat but their real genius is that away from the delighted shrieks of children playing, the often-crowded bike paths, and the noise of a basketball game, there are grassy trails to wander, wetland marshes to explore, and places where visitors may chance upon a family of ducks in the reeds or perhaps catch a glimpse of a peregrine falcon. And, perhaps what would most have pleased Mary Ellen Murphy, were she still alive, is the small beach where people can dip their toes in the water and watch the stars on a hot summer night.

Above: The rough textures and crisp edges of the granite terrace complement a planting of beach roses, switch grass, and dawn redwood.

Opposite: The Sumac Path, which climbs the west side of the Pier 1 mound, features native sumac species, as well as sassafras, chestnut oak, and native viburnum.

Left: The Pier 6 flower field offers a generous expanse of ox eye sunflower, Joe Pye weed, swamp milkweed, and queen of the prairie that create a compelling context for more urban elements like large-scale public art and skyline views.

Willis Avenue Community Garden
The Bronx

In 1995, when Bette Midler returned to live in New York, the "Divine Miss M" was appalled at the condition of the streets and neighborhood parks in Manhattan. As she said in an interview with *House Beautiful*, "I was so upset; I didn't sleep for weeks . . . People were throwing their garbage out the window, leaving their lunches on the ground. Finally, I realized I needed to actually do something—even if it meant picking up trash with my own two hands." Doing something meant recruiting her family and friends to help clear the trash.

This, in turn, led to the founding of the New York Restoration Project (NYRP) and an extraordinary effort to clean up 20,000 tons of garbage from Fort Tryon and Fort Washington Parks. From that grassroots begining, NYRP has become a powerful force in advocating and preserving community gardens and revitalizing green spaces in the city.

In 1999 a different kind of challenge arose when Mayor Rudolph Giuliani announced plans to sell 114 community gardens and vacant lots to developers as part of an effort to reduce a budget shortfall. NYRP went into action. Working with the Trust for Public Land and other non-profit garden coalitions, the group raised enough public awareness and money to save all of these gardens and open spaces. When NYRP took over the care and maintenance of 52 of them (the Trust for Public Land took responsibility for the remainder of the plots), it was the start of a new era and put the city on notice that outdoor neighborhood space is fundamental to the quality of urban life and that every community in New York City deserves its piece of green.

The NYRP website has images and descriptions of thriving and well-tended gardens in every borough. One example is Willis Avenue Community Garden in the Mott Haven section of the Bronx. Once a vacant and trash-filled eyesore, this 9,063 square-foot garden—encompassing four city lots—was originally founded in 1997 by members of the nearby Congregational Church of North New York and other local residents, and it was one of the community gardens saved in 1999 by NYRP.

A generous grant from the Perlman Family Foundation provided funds for an overhaul and refurbishment of the garden, including the construction of a new pergola, tool shed, steel picket fencing, twenty-four raised beds, and an expanded butterfly garden. The renovated garden was reopened in 2014, with two new patios, a mulched picnic area, a regraded lawn, and new plantings around the garden's border, pathways, and birch trees.

Preceding spread and left: Raised beds of vegetables and flowers are tended by neighborhood residents with support from the NYRP.

The garden provides a rare green space for neighborhood education and entertainment, and the community's largely Puerto Rican heritage is visible on a new casita, where two Puerto Rican flags hang on either side of the American flag. Traditionally, a casita, or "little house" is a one-story wood-frame shed structure popular in gardens for social gatherings in Puerto Rico. Here, the casita is a modular design, the creation of TEN

Left: Metal hoops can be covered to protect tender greens and lettuces in early spring.

Above: The casita is the perfect spot for a game of cards and conversation.

Arquitectos, that allows a community to choose how to assemble its lego-like building components to best fit the space and serve its needs. At Willis Avenue, the casita has become the social hub of the garden and provides a shaded meeting area, space for yoga and fitness classes, a place for a game of dominoes, and a bandstand for community events.

The garden is open from April to November, and NYRP meets regularly with the local garden committee to decide on perennial and annual planting choices, discuss problems, and prioritize tasks. In addition to local volunteer garden help, its operations team is on hand for regular maintenance and to assist with special projects such as tree pruning. It's a collaborative model that operates in all of NYRP gardens, and one that is transforming life outdoors in every borough.

Peggy Rockefeller Rose Garden

New York Botanical Garden

May and June are the best times to stop, stoop, and savor the roses in the Peggy Rockefeller Rose Garden. With more than 750 different roses and 2,700 plants, this profusion of colors, shapes, and fragrance makes for a heady experience. The colors run from pink and white at the north end to purple and orange at the south, with red and apricot at the main western entrance.

These show-stopping blooms encompass both historic and modern varieties—floribunda, grandiflora, musk, noisette, shrub, and hybrid tea—a living encyclopedia of roses. All are neatly labeled and organized with many of their names invoking royalty, historical figures, events, and celebrities. Be prepared to run into Mozart and Marilyn Monroe. Look out for Renoir or Queen Elizabeth, and there's no reason not to meet a delightful yellow rose named for Julia Child.

This expansive rose garden has faultless provenance. In 1916 Beatrix Farrand, Edith Wharton's niece and the leading American landscape designer of her day, was asked by Nathaniel Lord Britton, founder of the New York Botanical Garden (NYBG), to design a formal rose garden. Farrand picked out a slightly sloping triangular piece of land, thought to have been the site of a garden and pond on the Lorillard estate, which predated NYBG. She took as her inspiration a famous French garden, Roserai de L'Hay, which is a few kilometers south of Paris. The first garden to be devoted exclusively to roses, it was created in 1892 by the notable landscape architect and horticulturist Édouard André, and was an immediate sensation.

Sadly, Farrand's plans were never finished because of funding issues. The eighty-three beds and intersecting paths were laid out as she had specified, but the centerpiece of her garden—an elaborate wrought-iron gazebo, which appears to have been closely modeled on the helmeted dome designed by André for his French garden—was never erected. Also missing was the high lattice fencing, which Farrand intended to enclose the garden on all sides.

Over the years, the rose garden became one of the least-visited parts of NYBG. In 1985 Beth Straus, a board member and herself a passionate gardener, came across Farrand's original plans and persuaded her friend David Rockefeller to put up the money needed to do a renovation. By 1988, seventy-two years after it was first designed, Farrand's garden was finally completed, with new gates and the lattice fencing and gazebo executed exactly as specified in her plans. It was named in honor of Rockefeller's wife, who was a conservationist, enthusiastic gardener, and rose lover.

Today, following a further refurbishing in 2007, the garden offers visitors the chance to see a rare example of an early twentieth-century Farrand design. The garden is in bloom from May to October with a constant succession of roses ready to dazzle and delight. A visit here is a must for rose lovers, rose growers, and especially those who have given up the struggle to grow their own roses. After witnessing the seductive charm of these voluptuous beauties, they may even be tempted to try their luck one more time.

Preceding spread: The first flush of flowers in the Peggy Rockefeller Rose Garden reaches a peak in early June, just as the Kousa dogwoods on the surrounding slopes come into bloom.

Right: The iron fence around the Rose Garden provides protection against hungry rabbits as well as perfect purchase for climbing roses such as pale pink 'Leander' and the darker 'Parade'.

Above and right: Although *Rosa* Mon Petit Chou® exhibits the full, romantic flowers of old-fashioned shrub roses, it is a modern hybrid tea introduced by the Kordes Nursery of Germany. *Rosa* 'Will Scarlet' is a vigorous shrub that can be trained as a climber.

Left: *Rosa* 'Awakening', which clambers over the central gazebo, was discovered as a sport of the popular climbing rose 'New Dawn'. Rosarians tout its disease resistance, vigor, and repeat flowering.

The Cloisters
Fort Tryon Park

Most of the great medieval monasteries of Europe are long since gone, along with their cloistered gardens. But, for those who would like to take a step back in time and learn about the spirit and ethos of a medieval monastic garden, the Cloisters in Fort Tryon Park is the place to go.

The museum (a branch of the Metropolitan Museum of Art) is perched on a high hilltop in northern Manhattan with breathtaking views of the Hudson River. It has a superb collection of medieval works of art, including the world-famous Unicorn Tapestries, housed in a building that incorporates architectural fragments of Gothic and Romanesque abbeys. The cloisters evoke the atmosphere of medieval monastic life, and the color, texture, and fragrance of the plants in the cloisters draw their inspiration from the tapestries, stained glass, paintings, and decorative works of art on display.

There are three reconstructed cloisters with gardens. Surprisingly few historical records exist to give precise information about what would have been planted in a medieval cloister garden. We do know that medieval gardens were utilitarian endeavors—herbs were grown for medicinal purposes, plants were used as dyes, and fruit and vegetables were to be eaten. Tapestries of the period show enclosed greenswards carpeted with flowers, many of which had symbolic and allegorical meanings.

The Cloisters opened to the public in 1938, and the gardens were largely developed by two medieval art scholars, James Rorimer, who was the curator of the department of medieval art, and Margaret Freeman, a lecturer and curator at the museum. They studied old herbals, consulted medieval writers, such as Albertus Magnus and Walahfrid Strabo, the Abbot of Reichenau, were guided by Charlemagne's list of what was planted in his ninth-century imperial garden, and drew on three famous ninth-century sources—the Plan of St. Gall, Capitulare de Villis, and Strabo's Hortulus—to compile their plant list.

The Cuxa Cloister (recently renamed the Judy Black Garden at the Cuxa Cloister) is the focal point of the main-floor galleries. It is a reconstruction, about one-quarter the original size, of the Romanesque cloister from the Benedictine monastery of Saint Michel-de-Cuxa in the Spanish Pyrenees. Covered walkways with twelfth-century capitals enclose a square open-air garden, or to use the medieval term, garth. There is a fountain at the center and the space is divided into four quadrants, each with a grass plot and a pollarded crab apple tree, whose sour fruit would have been employed by the monks to make cider. The grass has a surprisingly shaggy look, but this is intentional since grass was cut with scythes in medieval times. An assortment of medieval herbs and modern cultivars—lavender, alyssum, angelonia, columbine, sage, hellebores, iris, and roses—border the paths, providing color and scent from early spring to late fall. In winter, the arcades are glassed in and the interior walkway turns into a conservatory, filled with pots of date palm, orange, rosemary, acanthus, and bay.

Preceding spread and right: In the Cuxa Cloister, the space is divided into four quadrants and flowers line the interior edges of the lawn, providing a continuous array of color from early spring through late fall.

Left: The beds of herb garden in the Bonnefont Cloister are intentionally divided into plant species with different functions, such as aromatic plants, dye plants, and kitchen and seasoning plants.

Above: The practice of espaliering fruit trees (flattening their branches) became popular in the seventeenth century. This method facilitated producing fruit within the walls of a courtyard and provided a decorative element to a solid wall, illustrated by this pear tree in the Bonnefont Cloister.

The Bonnefont Cloister is on the lower level of the museum, enclosed on two sides by arcades topped with marble capitals from the late thirteenth-century cloister of the Cistercian Abbey of Bonnefont-en-Comminges in southwestern France. It is a large herb garden with nineteen raised beds, bordered with wattle fences, and placed around a fifteenth-century Venetian wellhead. There are four quince trees in the center, and the beds are planted with 250 species of plants and herbs that would have been grown in the Middle Ages and are grouped and labeled according to their medieval uses—culinary, aromatic, magic, and medicinal. An espaliered pear tree, which would not have been found in a medieval garden, grows one of the outer walls. Who knows why it was added, but no matter, it blends well into its surroundings.

The Trie Cloister has the smallest and the most intimate garden, and its arcade incorporates late-fifteenth-century marble bases and capitals from monasteries in the Biggore region of France. Until recently, this garden was planted only with flowers shown in the Unicorn Tapestries, but since they are predominately spring flowers, the garden would peak by midsummer. A broader plant palette, drawing inspiration from more tapestries, has now been introduced to extend the bloom season. The new planting scheme is loose and informal, and it is intended to give the impression of a natural flowering meadow. The garden is divided into quadrants, and travertine pavers radiate from a central fountain. The beds are planted with low growing plant species, such as angel hair, fescue, creeping thymes, sea thrift, and Scottish harebell, with larger perennials and shrubs closer to the fountain.

Traditionally, the cloister was at the heart of monastic life and a place where the monks would read, sleep, walk, meditate, and make their gardens. All three of the gardens at the Cloisters invite us to step back in time and experience a way of life far removed from our own lives.

Right: Originally planted only with flowers depicted in the Unicorn Tapestries, the Trie Cloister was recently replanted with a broader plant palette to give it more year-round color interest.

Left: The Cuxa Cloister

High Line
Manhattan

Above grade in every way, the High Line
has been an unqualified triumph from the
day it opened in 2009. This structure, which
was declared obsolete thirty years ago, now
attracts more than six million visitors a
year and is the second most popular tourist attraction in New York, nipping at the
heels of the Metropolitan Museum of Art in
visitation.

The High Line was originally an elevated
rail line, built in the 1930s to move freight
close to the docks along the west side of
Manhattan. By 1980, with the decline of
waterfront trade, the trains had stopped
running, and it had become an abandoned
piece of industrial infrastructure. The
southern section, which ran from St. John's
Terminal at Houston Street to Gansevoort
Street in the meatpacking district, was dis-
mantled, leaving the remaining stretch from
Gansevoort Street to 34th Street a deserted
junkyard awaiting the wrecking ball.

In 1999 entrepreneur Robert Hammond and
freelance writer Joshua David, who both

lived near the High Line but had no previous experience in community action or urban planning, met at a community board hearing. Soon after, they formed Friends of the High Line to advocate for preserving the former railroad and reusing it as public open space. As David later remarked: "This is really like one of those great New York stories where two guys who didn't even know each other decided to save this giant piece of the city's history from oblivion."

At first, David and Hammond's idea to give New York a garden walkway in the sky seemed preposterous, even though the Promenade Plantée in Paris, which opened in 1993, was a compelling precedent. There were some differences—the Paris walkway was longer and wider than the High Line and was in a residential neighborhood —but they were not significant, and being able to point to this successful model was a valuable asset.

David and Hammond's first move was to ask photographer Joel Sternfeld to document the High Line. His images, taken over the course of a year, showed an untamed meadow-like space overgrown with weeds, and conveyed far better than any speech or written material the potential for its conversion into a public green space. In addition, David and Hammond displayed a genius for getting press, a talent for raising money, and an uncanny ability to attract the backing of influential friends. Gradually, the idea of saving the High Line gained momentum; and in 2004 an international juried competition was held and chose the design team of architects Diller Scofidio + Renfro, landscape architect James Corner Field Operations, and garden designer Piet Oudolf.

When the first section of the High Line opened, what immediately struck home was the visceral excitement of being thirty feet above the street—a perspective that completely alters the experience of the city. The walkway snakes among old industrial buildings, offering glimpses of the Hudson, rubbing up against the few tenements still almost close enough to touch,

Preceding spread: Planted with salvia and looking toward 20th Street, this section of the High Line is known as the Chelsea grasslands. The steel hoops in the foreground are part of a temporary art installation.

Right: The trunks of a group of birch trees seen through the foliage of a service-berry tree where the High Line heads north from 17th Street.

Left: A jutting overlook on the northern spur is planted with Pennsylvania sedge, alumwart, and Max Frei geraniums.

and jagging past the frenzy of new buildings springing up on either side. Some of the original tracks have been retained, and the walking surface consists of precast concrete planks that sometimes diverge and rise up or taper down to blend into the plantings. In some places, the path shrinks to a narrow foot bridge, in others it goes under cover, and at one point opens to a surprisingly wide patch of meadow.

Oudolf, who was in charge of planting design, is best known for choosing perennials and grasses that subtly relate to each other. The hallmark of his approach is sustainability and year-round interest. His plant selections for the High Line favored drought-tolerant, low-maintenance species, many of them grown within one hundred miles of New York, and his mix of grasses, flowering meadow plants, and woodland shrubs suggested a conscious effort to retain some of the unruly weed-like feeling of the High Line's former wilderness. A long linear park could be monotonous, but Oudolf keeps it lively by providing moments of drama and incorporating interesting and unexpected transitions of woodland, wetland, and grassland along the way. "I tried to get the look and feel of a wild garden, combined with a bit more order," he explains.

Gardening on the High Line presents special challenges, which have resulted in some changes to the original planting plan. Shallow beds, eighteen inches deep on average but in some places only eight inches, make it difficult for plants to survive intense winter cold. Head gardener Andi Pettis explains there has been some editing out of plants that simply did not thrive under the extreme wind conditions. "Wind is an exercise in giving up control, and we are working with new wind patterns in the park. We are continually adding plants, which are not all native to North America but which evoke a sense of place." Some of the plants that Oudolf selected have self-seeded and spread, and bur oaks, fifteen feet when planted, are now close to twenty-five feet high. New high-rise construction along the path has also affected growing conditions, adding both shade and reflected light. All of these factors, in

addition to the impact of huge crowds, makes for a continuing dialog between Oudolf's aesthetic and the living ecology of the High Line.

All three sections of the High Line are now open, and it stretches from the new Whitney Museum of American Art at Gansevoort Street to West 34th Street between 10th and 11th Avenues. Owned by the City of New York and maintained and operated by the Friends of the High Line, which provides more than 90 percent of its operating budget, the High Line's extraordinary popularity with both New Yorkers and tourists from all over

Three views of the northern spur taken (from left to right) in May, late August, and the end of September.

Overleaf: A grove of native maples shade a group of "peel up" benches, made of tropical hardwood with diagonal concrete risers. The art deco railings of the original railroad structure can be seen in the background.

the world shows no sign of abating. Art events and cultural programs for all ages abound. Attendance numbers are up every year, and during the summer months, the crowds of pedestrians, joggers, and baby carriages can at times seem overwhelming. In winter, the atmosphere is more tranquil but no less dynamic. Regardless of season, the High Line is a superb example of a successful contemporary urban landscape and offers a brilliant way to be outdoors and celebrate the city.

Above: A mass planting of Karl Foerster feather grass looking toward 20th Street.

Right: In late November, the berries of red spiked winterberry provide color and interest.

Left: A group of whitespire birch trees in a woodland area near the West 12th Street entrance.

Noguchi Museum Garden

Long Island City

"Through gardens, I came to a deeper awareness of nature and of stone," wrote Isamu Noguchi, one of the greatest and most inventive sculptors of the twentieth century. The son of a Japanese father and an American mother, Noguchi spent time in both countries as a child, traveled constantly all his life, and never lost the feeling of being an outsider. The quietness of his art is quite different from the work of most of his contemporaries, and a sense of not belonging, which drove his art and stayed with him all his life, also sets him apart.

Adhering to the Japanese tradition that there is no absolute division or distinction between art and craft, Noguchi was never content to be only a sculptor. He made stage sets for Martha Graham, designed furniture, created his much-celebrated paper Akari lanterns, and designed several gardens. He wanted to be remembered not for a particular body of work but rather for contributing "to an awareness of living."

Nowhere is this awareness more evident than in the museum and garden which he created in Astoria, Queens, to house and exhibit his work. That in the mid-1960s, he set up his studio in an industrial area of Queens and not in Lower Manhattan, was a sure indication that he was ahead of his time. It was here in 1975 where he decided to make a museum to show his sculpture. To do this, he purchased a former photo-engraving plant across the street. It was a two-story brick building, to which he added a cinderblock wing in 1981. Next, he acquired an adjoining gas station to make space for a garden. This gave him a triangular site, which he enclosed with a high wall for complete privacy. The museum and garden opened in 1985.

Preceding spread: Beneath the canopy of the katsura tree are *The Illusion of the Fifth Stone* (center), *Big Bang* (foreground), and *End Pieces* (left). Across the space is the entrance to Area 1 of the galleries.

Above: *Indian Dancer* (center) with *Practice Rocks in Placement* in the foreground.

Opposite: *Bench*.

Noguchi always intended that the garden, in addition to providing an outdoor setting for his larger pieces of stone sculpture, be an integral part of the museum whose official name is the Isamu Noguchi Foundation and Garden Museum. The garden is a continuation of the indoor space and contains twenty-three pieces of sculpture. Noguchi gave meticulous specifications for their placement, observing in his working notes: "The art of stone in a Japanese garden is that of placement. Its ideal does not deviate from that of nature except in providing a heightened appreciation."

A visitor enters the museum through the garden, and in the first major gallery space beyond the lobby, immediately sees a small clump of river birches, planted in an open, angled corner. The galleries flow into the walled garden, in the middle of which is a katsura tree, which is now almost forty feet high, its imposing canopy shading the garden far more extensively than when it was planted by Noguchi so many years ago. Clumps of bamboo soften the walls, over which English and Boston ivy have been trained to climb. There are three groupings of Japanese black pines, while other trees include weeping cherry, magnolia, Japanese holly, and silver birch. Closer to the ground are azaleas, boxwood, mounded junipers, vinca, and moss. Noguchi gave precise planting instructions, and nothing has changed except for the felling of one ailanthus tree. It grew so large that it became a safety hazard and was removed in 2008 during a major renovation to the museum and garden.

The plants and trees offer a marked contrast to the shape and texture of the outdoor sculpture, and the space in between is a critical element of Noguchi's design. Sharply angled concrete paths wind around beds of dark-gray trap rock, giving the appearance of flowing water. The story goes that while the garden was under construction, Noguchi happened to see a truck transporting a load of coarse gray pebbles for another unrelated job nearby. Liking their size and color, he decided to use identical ones in his own garden.

To a Western eye, the garden seems to draw its inspiration from a classic Japanese garden, where gravel is intentionally shaped into cloud-like contours and water is heard but often unseen. Here, the range in scale and materials and the positioning of sculpture give the viewer an intense awareness of nature but Noguchi's design is not that of a traditional Japanese garden. Meditative, playful, and filled with elegant shapes, it very much reflects his own aesthetic and should be understood the way he saw it: "A crossing where inward and outward meet, East and West."

Right: *Helix of the Endless* set against the spreading katsura tree along the path from Area 3.

160

From left: *Behind Inner Seeking Shiva Dancing*; Trees within the cinderblock enclosure of Area 1; *The Well (Variation on a Tsukubai)* in the foreground with *Behind Inner Seeking Shiva Dancing*,

Shakespeare Garden
Central Park

There was no plan for a Shakespeare garden in Frederick Law Olmsted and Calvert Vaux's original design for Central Park. Its immediate forebear, also never a part of their design, was a Victorian-style rock garden with the curious name "Garden of the Heart." This had been established in 1913 on part of the hilly terrain that leads to the Belvedere Castle, just north of 79th Street, on the west side of the park. With the tercentennial of Shakespeare's death approaching on April 23, 1916, Parks Commissioner Charles Stover came up with the idea to convert the rock garden into a Shakespeare garden in honor of the playwright.

The challenge of making a garden restricted to plant material mentioned in Shakespeare's plays and poetry was given to Edmond Bronk Southwick, who was the official entomologist of Central Park for almost thirty years. Known to have been a voracious reader and great Shakespeare lover, he is said to have accepted his assignment with great enthusiasm.

When the new garden, filled with columbine, primroses, rosemary, pansies, wormwood, quince, lark's heel, rue, eglantine, flax, thistle, and cowslips opened to the public, it was an immediate success. On April 2, 1916, the *New York Times* reported that "the fence around the garden is low and can be stepped over in any part but Dr. Southwick says that no one has ever intruded and that there has never been any demonstration there of the spirit of destruction which so often reveals itself in the New York urchin." Perhaps not, but sadly a marble bust of the bard in the garden was later vandalized and never replaced.

During its early years, the garden was looked after by Dr. Southwick and the Shakespeare Society. However, when the Society disbanded in 1929, the garden began to fall into disrepair. By the 1970s, like much of Central Park, it was overgrown, untended, and unkempt. When Shakespeare wrote in Henry IV "Now 'tis the spring and weeds are shallow-rooted. Suffer them now, and they'll o'ergrow the garden," he was referring to the king's enemies, but his lines describe perfectly the garden's demise.

Help arrived in 1975 when a group of volunteers stepped in to clean up the garden. In 1986 the Central Park Conservancy, with a grant from the Samuel and May Rudin Foundation, undertook a five-year restoration, appointing designers Bruce Kelly and David Varnell to replant and expand the borders, repave the paths, and install rustic benches and Chippendale-style fencing. Small bronze plaques with quotations from Shakespeare were also tucked in between the plants.

Today, the Shakespeare garden is a quiet enclave within Central Park. It winds up a steep hill, beginning at the steps of the Swedish Cottage, where there used to be a much-prized ancient mulberry tree, said to have been grafted from one planted by Shakespeare. Sadly, it was felled in 2006 by a violent summer storm. Each spring, the garden is home to a riotous display of bulbs. Come summer, the beds are planted with lilies, cone flowers, trumpet vine, bee balm, meadow rue, and, of course, roses. Although the plant palette is no longer exclusively Shakespearian, the garden is a haven for plant lovers, bird watchers, and, of course, for those wanting to brush up on Shakespeare.

Preceding spread and right: Rustic Chippendale-style fencing edges and defines the planting beds on either side of the stone steps leading to the upper level of the garden.

Above and opposite: In early spring the garden bursts into bloom with a mass of daffodils, evoking lines from *The Winter's Tale*:

"Daffodils, that come before the swallows dare, and take the winds of March with beauty."

Brooklyn Botanic Garden

The history of Brooklyn Botanic Garden (BBG) goes back to the last decade of the nineteenth century when talk of creating a botanic garden and arboretum in Brooklyn first began. Little progress was made until 1905, when Alfred Tredway White, an enlightened developer and philanthropist, agreed to contribute the necessary funding. A bill authorizing the city to establish and maintain a botanical garden was approved the next year by the New York State Legislature, and in 1910 Brooklyn Botanic Garden was established on twenty-two acres of rubble-strewn and boulder-filled land (later increased to fifty-five acres) adjacent to Prospect Park. Olmsted Brothers was retained to lay out and grade the site and, in 1912, Harold Caparn was hired as landscape architect, with McKim, Mead & White chosen to design an administration building and palm house.

Today, visitors to BBG have a wealth of gardens and plant collections to explore. From the Eastern Parkway entrance, the first is the Osborne Garden— a semi-formal Italianate-style garden with ten wisteria-hung pergolas that was designed in 1935 by Caparn. In spring, daffodils, pansies, and tulips bloom, followed by crab apples and cherries, which gradually give way to azaleas, rhododendrons, wisterias, and dogwood. Evergreens and flowering fruit trees shade the walkways while rhododendrons and azaleas line the paths; on the west side is a boulder wall with bulb and herbaceous plantings.

Nearby is the Cranford Rose Garden, which first opened in 1928 and has always been a favorite attraction. Also designed by Caparn, it is lush, romantic, and old-fashioned, with fifteen rectangular beds set in a one-acre rectangle and separated by panels of grass. Enclosed by a white lattice fence, the garden is home to more than one thousand species and varieties of roses, both old and modern, including wild species, old garden roses, hybrid teas, grandifloras, floribundas, polyanthas, hybrid perpetuals, climbers, ramblers, and miniatures. Some of the original roses are still growing in the garden today.

Also close by is the Japanese Hill-and-Pond Garden, BBG's best-known destination. The decision to make a Japanese-style garden at the beginning of the twentieth century was a reflection of the vogue for all things Japanese at that time. The garden, which opened in 1915, cost all of $13,000 (another gift from the generous Mr. White) and was the first Japanese-inspired garden created in an American public garden. The designer, recommended by the Japanese Consul General, was Takeo Shiota, who had arrived in the United States in 1907 with the stated ambition to create "a garden more beautiful than all others in the world."

Japanese gardens are designed to mirror nature—particularly Japan's rocky coastline and mountainous landscape—and to use trees, plants, and structures on a scale that creates an impression of greater space. Shiota used motifs from many Japanese gardens in his stroll garden, which features two waterfalls and a series of artificial hills surrounding a pond in which there is an island. His architectural elements included wooden bridges, stone lanterns, a viewing pavilion, a torii (a red gate-like structure), and a Shinto shrine. Many of the larger trees—white pine, American beech, and bald cypress—are native to North America and were already planted before the site was developed into a Japanese garden.

Preceding spread: The Japanese Hill-and-Pond Garden, designed by Takeo Shiota, opened in 1915.

Right: The Cranford Rose Garden contains thousands of specimens, including old garden varieties, species roses, and modern hybrids, and is inter-planted with annuals and perennials that attract beneficial insects.

Left: The Japanese Hill-and-Pond Garden is a blend of the ancient hill-and-pond style and the more recent stroll-garden style, in which various landscape features are gradually revealed along winding paths.

Simplicity and harmonious asymmetry are important principles in Japanese garden design. Although a Japanese garden may look natural, it is anything but, and BBG's is no exception. Some of the pines are pruned and trained to look old and windswept while other trees and shrubs are tightly clipped to represent hills and clouds. Evergreen plants (especially pines) predominate and symbolize permanence, while brightly colored flowering plants, such as Japanese iris, wisteria, bamboo, tree peonies, and azaleas, are used with restraint. Most of the workers Shiota employed were local Italian laborers and stoneworkers. Scholars have noted that the waterfalls in the garden bear a strong resemblance to the grottoes and stonework found in classical Italian gardens, but since this is Brooklyn and not Japan, this idiosyncrasy is part of the garden's charm.

BBG's indoor plant collection is housed in the Steinhardt Conservatory complex, which is made up of several connected pavilions. There is an aquatic house, which is home to a large orchid collection as well as a variety of tropical and subtropical aquatic and wet-environment plants from around the world. Another gallery contains the biggest collection of bonsai in America. Stairs lead down to three more greenhouses—a desert pavilion, a temperate pavilion, and, largest of all, a tropical pavilion. This gallery occupies 6,000 square feet under glass, recreating a tropical rainforest with waterfalls and streams, and housing plants and trees from the Amazon basin, African rainforest, and tropical eastern Asia.

Beyond the main building, a magnificent sweep of more than forty thousand deep-blue Spanish bluebells dazzles the woodland garden every May. Even more dramatic is the bloom of the garden's ornamental cherry trees (usually from the end of April into May). An annual two-day cherry blossom festival, held at the peak of the flowering season, is the garden's most popular event, attracting huge numbers of visitors eager to admire the more than two hundred trees in the garden's extensive collection. But, for those less concerned with botanical drama, BBG is a rewarding garden to visit in any and every season.

Above and right: The Japanese Hill-and-Pond Garden features artificial hills contoured around a pond, a waterfall, and an island, along with carefully placed rocks.

Overleaf: More than forty thousand bluebells (*Hyacinthoides hispanica* 'Excelsior') are planted under a mature stand of oak, birch, and beech trees.

Madison Square Park

Manhattan

Madison Square Park is one of the city's success stories. It fell on hard times in the 1980s, and its recovery and transformation into one of the city's most vibrant green spaces were due to the efforts of local business leaders. Thanks to their leadership, Madison Square Park has become the nexus of the Flatiron district and one of the liveliest parks in the city.

The park, named for James Madison, fourth president of the United States, sits on 6.2 acres of open space above the intersection of Fifth Avenue and Broadway. Designated as public space by the first city charter in 1686, the land was used as a potter's field and then as part of an arsenal before it became a park in 1847. New York was moving northward, and the neighborhood was becoming a desirable place to live—Theodore Roosevelt, Edith Wharton, and Winston Churchill's mother, Jennie Jerome, were all born in this part of the city.

Originally not much more than a large lawn, the park was redesigned in 1870 by landscape architect William Grant and Ignatz Pilat, an

Austrian gardener who had worked as a horticultural assistant to Frederick Law Olmsted on Central Park. They introduced curving paths lined with benches, open areas of lawn, a large fountain, and an array of deciduous trees. The park also became a popular repository for statues and monuments honoring politicians and veterans, most notably, the seated bronze figure of William Henry Seward and the monument to Civil War Admiral David Farragut.

A thriving area at the turn of the twentieth century, the Madison Square neighborhood declined over the succeeding decades. Finally, in the 1990s Metropolitan Life and New York Life, whose headquarters were built on the east side of the park in the early 1900s, and Danny Meyer, president of the Union Square Hospitality Group, launched the Campaign for Madison Square Park. Needing a parent organization to hold the funds, they worked in partnership with the City Parks Foundation, and in 1997, a $6 million four-year restoration program got underway.

Preceding spread: Curved beds filled with shade-loving plants such as hydrangea and hosta are Madison Square Park's signature design.

Above left: Monument to Civil War Admiral David Farragut by Augustus Saint-Gaudens on a base designed by Stanford White.

Above center and right: A profusion of summer roses along the paths.

Cracked asphalt and broken benches were repaired, trees were pruned, and a reflecting pool and dog run were added. Lynden Miller was hired to be in charge of landscaping, but the schedule did not allow time for detailed drawings. "I did the design in my head and it was unlike anything I've done before or since," she recalls. The idea was to create a design with many planting areas. Miller underplanted perennials in large groupings under shrubs and used very few annuals. Given the shade, she relied heavily on hydrangeas, holly, and hostas, and she remembers making decisions about where to place the plants even as they came off the delivery trucks. It may have been a rushed job but the results were impressive. When the park re-opened in June 2001, the flower beds that wrap around the perimeter of the park and frame the statuary were a rich mix of shrubs, small trees, and sturdy perennials.

Left: Oakleaf hydrangeas provide summer blooms and fall foliage interest throughout the park.

Right: The Flatiron Building is one of a number of landmark structures on the perimeter of the park.

Overleaf: A parterre style planting features a range of annuals in front of the original Shake Shack.

In 2003 the Madison Square Park Conservancy was incorporated as a not-for-profit organization with a stated mission to make "a bright, beautiful, and active public park." The central lawn is a venue for musical and cultural events, programs for children, and multi-media contemporary art installations. Through Mad Sq. Hort, the Conservancy has developed a tree succession plan and a program of planting species collections of five perennial genera: daffodils (the New York State flower), hydrangeas, redbuds, camellias, and winter-blooming witch hazels. Today the park, which attracts more than 60,000 visitors on weekdays in the summer, is a constant hub of activity and a welcome verdant space in one of New York's most revitalized neighborhoods.

Brooklyn Grange
Brooklyn Navy Yard

High above New York, a quiet revolution is taking place on urban rooftops. Time was that roof gardens were the privileged enclave of a few well-heeled urban dwellers. Such gardens still flourish, but today the roof has become a new frontier for urban gardening. There will always be New Yorkers who lovingly tend to small pots of herbs on their window sills and take pride in cultivating a single tomato vine perched on the rung of a fire escape, but now there is also a new generation of imaginative, ambitious gardeners using roofs—usually on top of large commercial buildings—to grow vegetables and fruit, make compost, breed chickens, and even keep bees.

Green roofs use plants and flowers to provide insulation, create a habitat for local wildlife, help control runoff, and put more oxygen into the atmosphere. Designing and maintaining a high-in-the-sky vegetable garden is not so very different from designing and maintaining a rose garden in that it takes passion, commitment, time, and cash. However, making it a financially viable commercial venture is a considerably more sophisticated challenge.

In 2009 a group of four New Yorkers banded together to do something quite unprecedented. They were determined to build an organic rooftop vegetable farm to provide local produce for their community, change the way people think about food and urban agriculture, and make this endeavor a self-supporting enterprise. Empty roofs may be the last bastion of affordable New York real estate but finding one whose structure can support the weight of more than one million pounds of soil is not easy. Led by Ben Flanner, these young urban pioneers searched long and hard for suitable space. They gave up their indoor jobs, took out loans, contributed their own money, and persuaded investors to get involved in a new kind of urban agriculture.

Today, Brooklyn Grange, which has two locations and a total farming area of 2.5 acres, is the largest green roof farm in the country. Despite its name, the first site was actually in Queens, on top of a 43,000 square-foot roof that borders Astoria and Long Island City. The second site, which opened two years later in 2012, is atop the 65,000 square-foot roof of Building 3 in the Brooklyn Navy Yard. Together, these locations produce over 50,000 pounds of organically grown vegetables each year, house New York City's largest apiary with more than thirty beehives yielding approximately 1,500 pounds of honey annually, and are home to some very fetching resident chickens. Vegetables, all organic, are sold weekly at two neighborhood markets in Long Island City and Greenpoint and to a large number of local restaurants.

Not only are these statistics remarkable, but the know-how and savvy of Flanner and his co-founders is more than impressive. For starters, the technical challenge of setting up a green roof growing system on such a large scale involves obtaining building permits, employing cranes to lift the earth, and being knowledgeable about soil, drainage, layout, and nutrients in a rooftop growing environment. And, this is all in addition to the planting, growing, picking, and distribution of crops.

Only vegetables with shallow root systems can be grown at the Grange's two sites, where the beds are 8 to 12 inches deep. These include lots of

Preceding spread: Brooklyn Grange's rooftop farm in the Brooklyn Navy Yard.

Right: Crops, including several cultivars of kale seen here, are protected by taller sunflowers that act as windbreaks on the breezy roof.

different salad greens—from spicy baby mustards to tender young lettuces and peppery arugula—and more than forty varietals of tomatoes, peppers, kale, chard, chicories, ground cherries, eggplants, Bok choy, herbs, carrots, turnips, radishes, and beans.

The specially designed green roof soil drains well, and the farm uses mulch to help retain water. One of the favorites is cocoa husks, the waste product of a neighboring chocolate business in the Navy Yard. The husks are lightweight, nitrogen rich, and free.

Brooklyn Grange has thirteen full-time employees and more than forty seasonal part-time staff. It is thriving financially, offers a replicable model for sustainable urban gardening, and has a strong community focus with workshops and special events throughout the year. Visitors to this urban farm discover a giant, dynamic, and beautiful vegetable garden that is a sky-high success.

Above: The iconic New York water tank is original to the nineteenth-century building.

Right: Microgreens—shoots of edible plants—are grown in the greenhouse all year. This program generates "off-season" revenue and keeps the space actively used after the spring seedlings are transplanted to the field.

Wave Hill

The Bronx

Visitors to Wave Hill in Riverdale find it hard to believe they are in a public garden since the grounds have all the charm and ambience of the private estate that it once was. A municipal garden unlike any other, it has, as painter and gardener Robert Dash astutely observed, "Absolutely no institutional aesthetic."

The garden is approached by a pathway that leads from a small parking area (formerly the site of a tennis court) to a large expanse of lawn. On the far left is one of two magnificent copper beeches and more directly ahead are a bald cypress and an imposing dawn redwood. In the distance one can see a substantial nineteenth-century house. Ahead an elegant pergola is centered on a balustrade that runs the length of an Italianate terrace. It is covered with with two varieties of kiwi vines, and throughout the summer, large pots are massed around its decorative stuccoed pillars. From the terrace, there is a magnificent view of the Hudson river with the Palisades stretching far beyond. Times Square seems a million miles away.

Wave Hill House was built in 1843 by William Lewis Morris. In 1866 he sold the property to publisher William H. Appleton, who enlarged the house, improved the grounds, and leased out the house from time to time. Two of his more notable tenants were Mark Twain and Theodore Roosevelt. Years later, Toscanini also joined this distinguished roster of renters. In 1903 George W. Perkins, who owned the adjoining property, purchased Wave Hill House. He hired Albert Millard, a gardener trained in Vienna, to work with him on the layout of the gardens, grading the land, planting rare trees and shrubs, adding greenhouses and terraces, and creating a rose garden and a rock garden. Perkins also played a pivotal role in halting the development of the Palisades and securing the views of forested land on the far side of the river.

By 1953 development was changing the rural feel of Riverdale. Large apartment houses were springing up and the ultimate assault was a proposal for a shopping center in a wooded residential area close to the river and Wave Hill. A group of local residents led by Gilbert Kerlin, a neighbor of the Perkins family, formed the Riverdale Community Planning Association to wage an all-out campaign to pass a rezoning plan to prohibit large-scale development in the historic section of Riverdale and mandate a gradual transition from the older single-family houses near the river to the high-rise apartments and commercial buildings closer to the Henry Hudson Parkway. The association won and, in 1954, the largest rezoning measure in New York City's history was approved. It was a watershed victory for preservation, and without it, Wave Hill, as we know it today, would not exist.

In 1960 the Perkins family gave their twenty-eight-acre property to the city. It took another five years and a lot of help from Robert M. Morgenthau, the U.S. Attorney for New York and a Riverdale resident, to resolve Wave Hill's tax status and establish its designation as a not-for-profit entity. A public-private partnership was formed to manage the property, with Kerlin becoming Wave Hill's first chairman.

Preceding spread: The vine-covered pergola creates a shaded seating area overlooking the Hudson River.

Right: Lily pond in the aquatic garden.

Left: The flower garden in front of the conservatory in mid summer with daylilies, Annabelle and lacecap hydrangeas, and tansy in bloom.

The board hired Marco Polo Stufano as director of horticulture in 1967, and he worked at Wave Hill for thirty-three years in what he calls, "my first and only job." Remaking the garden was a long, slow process. Funds were scarce, and over the years Stufano, with the help of curator John Nally, did everything from clearing the weeds to laying steps, rebuilding and stocking the greenhouses, planting trees, and creating individual gardens. An adventurous gardener, Stufano loved to experiment with unusual plant combinations and was willing to try out any plant he came across. He understood that it takes time to establish a garden and that it pays not to rush. When he retired in 2001, Stufano left behind a mature plantsman's garden, now ably cared for by Louis Bauer and a staff of seven gardeners.

For visitors to Wave Hill, the logical first stop is the flower garden on the right side of the main lawn. It has the feel of a 1920s garden and is enclosed on three sides by a Chippendale-style cedar fence. Once a formal rose garden with grass paths, the space is now divided into four sections, intersected by two axial paths, and eight square beds filled with a mass of old-fashioned perennials and shrubs. Extra drama during summer months comes with the addition of hot-house exotics and unusual annuals. The beds are always full of visual surprise and alluring plant combinations, and this garden is a showpiece.

An adjacent conservatory greenhouse is stocked with succulents, cacti, and tropical plants. Behind it is a herb garden, a dry garden, and an alpine collection displayed in a group of stone troughs. Further up the hillside, Stufano has made a wild garden on the site of what was formerly a rock garden. He felt that it called for a casual look and filled the rocks and boulders with bulbs and woody plants arranged in a loose but controlled manner. Over time, self-seeders have spread prolifically and the garden emanates a free full-blown charm. Appearances, however, can be deceptive and, as Bauer explains, "This may look simple and natural, but the wild garden takes a lot of work."

There is much else to see at Wave Hill—an aquatic garden, a rustic gazebo, an elliptical garden, wonderful trees, and a series of paths that meander through the woods close to the river. Whether coming by car or public transportation, Wave Hill is a destination that requires time and effort to reach, but curiously this slight hurdle adds to the pleasure of a visit. And when a visitor does arrive, the garden, all giving, makes only one demand: slow down! This is not a garden to be rushed. To fully appreciate Wave Hill, it is essential to allow enough time to wander, savor, and absorb all it has to offer.

Above: One of two rustic Chippendale-style benches in the flower garden. Although the wood has been replaced three times, these benches date to the era when this was a private rose garden.

Right: Four mounds of box mark the intersection of the brick and bluestone paths that traverse the flower garden.

Left: A gravel path interspersed with stone steps winds through through a mass of alium, columbine, and *Hesperis matronalis* in the wild garden to the pavilion above.

Above: Weeping American white pine trees are part of the connifer collection at the north end of the garden.

Left: The wild garden
in spring with native
American dogwood and
Exochorda macanthra in
bloom.

West Side Community Garden
Manhattan

This garden had its origins in 1975 when a group of parents from PS 166 and other local residents took a stand against urban blight in their neighborhood. The focus of their anger was an 89,000-square-foot lot between 89th and 90th Streets and Amsterdam and Columbus Avenues, known as "strip city" because car thieves used it to dump stolen cars after stripping off the more desirable parts. Some buildings had been torn down, others had squatters living in them, and there was garbage and trash everywhere. This band of neighborhood activists went to work to remove the tons of debris and, having cleaned up the area, they got permission from their local community board to put up a fence and turn the space into a community garden.

By 1982, when the city selected a developer to construct housing on the site, the same neighborhood group, which had now become a membership organization, was determined to save at least some portion of their garden.

They met with the city and the developer and, with backing from their local community planning board, formed a coalition with the Trust for Public Land and other organizations advocating for open space. In 1989, after two years of negotiations, an agreement was reached, whereby a deed for a 16,000-square-foot site for a public neighborhood garden was conveyed by the city through the Trust for Public Land to the community, making it, according to current president, Jackie Bukowski, the first community group in New York to own its own garden.

Under the agreement, half the cost of making the garden would be paid by the developer, with cost of ongoing maintenance to be assumed by the neighborhood group, by now incorporated as a non-profit organization. Landscape designer Terry Schnadelbach worked with the community to come up with a garden design incorporating flowerbeds, arbors, pergolas, and a sheltered terraced amphitheatre. There are grass walks, benches, a community herb bed, six children's plots, and more than eighty flower and vegetable beds assigned to individual members for cultivation.

A good time to visit is in mid-to-late April when the West Side Community Garden holds its annual tulip festival, and people come from all over the city to see the multi-colored display of more than 15,000 tulips, all planted by volunteers. Later in the summer, the garden is a riot of annuals and vegetables, grown mostly from seed in a greenhouse on the grounds of the Cathedral of St. John the Divine. Members of the West Side Community Garden pay modest annual dues and are expected to contribute at least four hours a week to the garden. There are no paid gardeners and all the work is done by volunteers, even down to the opening and closing of the gates. The organization is extremely active, scheduling garden maintenance, planning garden events—there is a Shakespeare festival, and various music and movie events are scheduled throughout the summer—holding fundraisers, and applying for foundation grants. This vibrant attractive community garden is a shining example of how local involvement has transformed a temporary community space into a permanent and rightfully lauded public resource.

Preceding spread: A pergola shelters a bench along the perimeter wall.

Right: Raised beds throughout the garden are first planted in the spring with tulips and then filled with summer annuals.

208

Left: The garden can be entered from both 89th and 90th Streets. It offers flower displays, individual planting beds, children's plots, community events, and a place to sit, read, and relax.

Above: Fringed tulips are just one of the many varieties planted every year.

The Battery

According to the popular song, "The Bronx is up and the Battery's down." But for many years, the Battery, a twenty-five-acre park at the tip of Manhattan was "down" not only because of its location but also because it was neglected. This all changed in 1994 when Elizabeth Barlow Rogers, then president of the Central Park Conservancy, suggested to her friend Warrie Price that she replicate the private-public partnership model that was so successful at Central Park and establish a similar conservancy for Battery Park, as it was then called. Now, it has gone back to its historic name of The Battery.

A master plan for the park had been drawn up in the 1980s, but it was never implemented, and establishing a conservancy was thought to be the best way to revitalize the area. Unlike Central Park, where the Conservancy's only partner is the city, The Battery comes under the jurisdiction of city, state, and federal government, Such layers of bureaucracy might have deterred many people but not Price, who came to the task with a background in community-based planning.

When she arrived on the scene, The Battery was little more than a pass-through route to the embarkation point for ferries to the Statue of Liberty. A tangle of circuitous pathways snaked around a few sparse plots of exhausted grass that were heavily shaded by a desultory grove of London plane trees. The waterfront was dominated by parking spaces reserved for city and federal officials. "Cars on our historic waterfront! Can you believe it?" Price asks with mock drama in her voice. "Of course they had to go."

And they did, with Price sending officialdom the clear message that she meant business. Now, more than twenty years later, the Battery Park Conservancy (BPC) has implemented an ambitious master plan and raised $48 million in private funding. This has leveraged $92 million more in grants and public funds. Price's initial masterstroke was hiring the Dutch plantsman Piet Oudolf. Later, he was chosen as horticultural designer of the High Line, but when Price selected him, he was not a familiar name in this country.

Oudolf is best known for using swaths of grasses mixed with drifts of perennials, chosen for their shape, color, hardiness, year-long interest, and for the way they relate to each other. "I don't want to copy nature but to give a feeling of nature," he explains. For The Battery, he designed a series of beds along a promenade spanning the 1500-foot length of waterfront, where he combined 114 varieties of hybrid perennials and native plants. No annuals are used and it is a sustainable planting scheme that requires little watering. Serpentine granite benches, ingeniously recessed into the sides of the beds, offer a delightful vantage point to view the sweep of the harbor. The gardens were opened in December 2001, and three years later they were formally dedicated as "Gardens of Remembrance," honoring the promenade as an evacuation route on 9/11.

Phase two of Oudolf's plan was to redesign the 57,000-square foot shade area called the Bosque. The London plane trees, now pruned and limbed up, preside over twenty beds filled with a subtle mix of rugged prairie and woodland perennials that complement and contrast with the sun-loving plants in the Gardens of Remembrance.

Preceding spread: London plane trees in the Bosque.

Right: View of the New Jersey skyline from the Gardens of Remembrance with coneflower Echinacea and switch grass in the foreground.

Left: A mass of native plants, including foam flower and pink wild sweet William encircle the labyrinth.

Above: A row of swiss chard at the urban farm.

An unforeseen setback came in 2012, when Hurricane Sandy devastated much of the Battery with saltwater flooding. More than thirty trees, most of them London planes, were lost. Price and her team revitalized the wooded area, planting sixty new trees—tulip trees, willow, pin, and swamp white oaks, and a selection of under-story trees (redbud, dogwood and fringe trees)—all native varieties better able to resist future flooding. In addition to the Oudolf gardens, The Battery now boasts a labyrinth, an open grass oval area, a carousel, and even an urban farm, which grows everything from radishes to tomatoes and carrots to kale, sending its produce to three local schools and two food banks.

The southernmost tip of Manhattan is once again a vital vibrant green space. Under Price's aegis, The Battery is no longer down!

Above: Hosta 'blue angel' is planted along the path to the East Coast Memorial, which honors those who lost their lives in the Atlantic Ocean during World War II.

Opposite: The labyrinth, designed by Camino de Paz, is composed of seven rings of lawn edged with granite blocks. It was commissioned by BPC to honor the first anniversary of 9/11.

Overleaf: View from the Gardens of Remembrance over New York harbor.

New York's Smallest Public Garden

Manhattan

On 56th Street between 9th and 10th Avenues, a large and well-marked bump in the street slows down traffic almost to a halt. On the right hand side is a continually changing year-round garden display in front of the building at 424 West 56th Street. There is no proof that this is the smallest public garden in New York, but this exuberant creation in full view of the street is a likely candidate.

The creator is David Scalza, an artist who has lived on the first floor of this building for twenty years. His garden began about fifteen years ago when he made and placed window boxes outside his window. Filling the space beneath the window boxes came next, and Scalza gradually began to add pots, topiary, statuary, and an ever-changing assortment of found objects—more plants in the summer and more fanciful assemblages during the winter months.

Scalza does all the work himself. "The garden changes according to my mood," he says. "It used to be more picturesque, but now I've gone more rustic." Over the years, some objects have been broken or stolen but this doesn't deter Scalza. In fact, he has gone on to create a much larger garden behind his own and two adjoining buildings. Alas, that garden, not on the street, is by invitation only. However, his delightful street-side assemblage is there for all to see.

Gardens to Visit

Abby Aldrich Rockefeller
Sculpture Garden
Museum of Modern Art
11 West 53rd Street
New York, NY 10019
www.moma.org

The Battery
State Street and Battery Place
New York, NY 10004
www.thebattery.org

Brooklyn Botanic Garden
990 Washington Avenue
Brooklyn, NY 11225
www.bbg.org

Brooklyn Bridge Park
1 Water Street
Brooklyn, NY 11201
www.brooklynbridgepark.org

Brooklyn Grange
Brooklyn Navy Yard
Building 3
Clinton and Flushing Avenue
Brooklyn, NY 11205
www.brooklyngrangefarm.com

Carl Schurz Park
86th Street and East End Avenue
New York, NY 10028
www.carlschurzpark.org
www.nycparks.gov

Central Park
Conservatory Garden
Fifth Avenue and 104th Street
Shakespeare Garden
West Drive at 79th Street
www.centralparknyc.org
www.nycparks.gov

The Cloisters
99 Margaret Corbin Drive
Fort Tryon Park
New York, NY 10040
www.metmuseum.com

Franklin D. Roosevelt
Four Freedoms Park
1 FDR Four Freedoms Park
Roosevelt Island, NY 10044
www.fdrfourfreedomspark.org

Green-Wood
500 25th St
Brooklyn, NY 11232
www.green-wood.com

Heather Garden
Stan Michels Promenade
Fort Tryon Park
www.forttryonparktrust.org/
sites/heather-garden

High Line
Gansevoort Street and
Washington Street
New York, NY 10011
www.thehighline.org

Madison Square Park
Fifth Avenue and 23rd Street
New York, NY 10010
www.madisonsquarepark.org

New York Botanical Garden
Enid A. Haupt Conservatory
Native Plant Garden
Peggy Rockefeller Rose Garden
2900 Southern Boulevard
Bronx, New York 10458
www.nybg.org

New York Chinese
Scholar's Garden
Snug Harbor Cultural Center
and Botanical Garden
4 Second Avenue
Staten Island, NY 11232

Noguchi Museum Garden
9-01 33rd Road
Queens, NY 11106
www.noguchi.org

Paley Park
3 East 53rd Street
New York, NY 10022

Wave Hill
649 West 249th Street
Bronx, NY 10471
www.wavehill.org

West Side Community Garden
123 West 89th Street
New York, NY 10024
www.westsidecommunity
garden.org

Willis Avenue Community Garden
378 Willis Avenue
Bronx, NY 10454
www.nyrp.org

World Trade Center Memorial Garden
180 Greenwich Street
New York, NY 10001
www.911memorial.org

Please check websites for hours as some gardens are open seasonally.

First published in the United States by
The Monacelli Press.

Photographs by Mick Hales except

  Franklin D. Roosevelt Four Freedoms
  Park 26–27, 28–29

  New York Botanical Garden 88–89,
  92–93, 94

  Samuel G. White 180 left, 183

Library of Congress Control Number
2017962332

ISBN 978-158093-480-0

Design: Susan Evans, Design per se

Printed in China

The Monacelli Press
6 West 18th Street
New York, New York 10011

Acknowledgments

There are many people to thank: Mick Hales, whose willingness to put in long days to come up with great images never flagged; Elizabeth White, whose editorial skills, patience, and good humor have crafted this book every step of the way; and Susan Evans for designing this book with such care and sensibility. I also want to thank Gregory Long for his insights and encouragement, Betsy Smith for opening doors, and Sandy McClatchy for giving me a title. And I am indebted for their help to Randy Bourscheidt, Sarah Gund, Frances X. Paulo Huber, Timothy Husband, Elise Lufkin, Rob McQuilkin, Lynden Miller, Patricia Nadosy, Warrie Price, and Michael Shulan.

I am grateful to everyone who helped me uncover vanished history and put me in touch with people I needed to reach. Many thanks to the staff and gardeners at so many of New York's public gardens who took time out of their busy schedules to show me around, answer my questions, and so graciously accommodated Mick's photography schedule. In particular, I would like to thank Susannah Abbate, Edward Ames, Cub Barrett, Louis Bauer, Janine Biunno, Jacqueline Bukowski, Michael Carter, Joseph Charap, Anna Dolgov, Janelle Grace, Madeline Grimes, Michael Hagen, Jennifer Hoppa, Edith Kean, Sean Kiley, Caleb Leach, Stephanie Lucas, Stephen Martin, Deborah Marton, Karen Meyerhoff, Keats Myer, Anastasia Cole Plakias, Andi Pettis, Jan Ramirez, Elizabeth Reina-Longoria, David Scalza, Marco Polo Stufano, Kirstin Swanson, Matthew Urbanski, Banford Weissman, and Marilyn Young.